SLAVERY

AND

THE REMEDY;

OR,

PRINCIPLES AND SUGGESTIONS

FOR A

REMEDIAL CODE.

BY

SAMUEL NOTT.

"Bonds make free, be they but righteous bonds.   Freedom enslaves, if it be an unrighteous freedom." — PAGE 28.

SIXTH EDITION;

WITH A REPLY AND APPEAL TO

EUROPEAN ADVISERS.

NEGRO UNIVERSITIES PRESS
NEW YORK

Originally published in 1859
by Crocker and Brewster

Reprinted from a copy in the collections
of the Brooklyn Public Library

Reprinted 1969 by
Negro Universities Press
A DIVISION OF GREENWOOD PRESS, INC.
NEW YORK

SBN 8371-2722-X

PRINTED IN UNITED STATES OF AMERICA

ADVERTISEMENT

TO THE SIXTH EDITION.

THIS work was first published at the beginning of the year 1856. The Presidential Election at the close of that year and the Decision of the Supreme Court in the case of Dred Scott, gave occasion in the fourth and fifth editions for additional illustration of the principles which must govern the relations of the African and European races in the United States.

The several editions have been received with so much favor by some of the largest slave-holders, and by many eminent citizens and statesmen both North and South, as to encourage the belief that the work is not unfitted to its high purpose of engaging the Slave-holding States in their special duty to the African race, and of uniting the Free States in the only position for rendering effectual as well as acceptable aid.

With the deepest assurance that its principles and methods are such as Christian Philanthropy requires, we submit them as the true answer to the rebukes and demands of Foreign Societies and the Foreign Press, with such preliminary illustrations as European instances afford.

It will be found that we do not object to the interest taken in our affairs on the other side the Atlantic. We claim only, abroad as at home, that every proposal shall duly regard actual conditions and relations — shall seek a possible, substantial, and permanent good. He is our "neighbor," the wide world over, who even *advises* the "mercy" suited to our need.

REPLY AND APPEAL.

THE original design of "Slavery and the Remedy" was to fix the attention of the people of the United States upon the essential points of the question of slavery, now that the African race is to be regarded as settled in the land.

In executing this design we distinguished slavery, as a fact, from the proposal to enslave. Discarding the proposal, but requiring the fact to be treated as a fact, with due regard to actual conditions and relations, we turned the question from mere abolition and mere slavery to the well-being of the enslaved; and proposed a Remedial Code, as we believed, suited to the case and worthy to satisfy the conscience and philanthropy of the country by its beneficent character and tendency. At the same time we asserted the irresponsibility of the United States as a National Government, and the responsibility of each separate slaveholding State alone; and that the Free States, individually and socially, had no other obligation in the matter but to aid the work of well-being by all possible means of wisdom and good will.

In this edition we extend our design, and offer the

principles and methods of this work to the consideration of those abroad, whose earnest remonstrances and appeals demand of the United States the abolition of slavery. The letters we receive, and the whole expression of the Foreign Press, seem to us utterly indiscriminate of facts and proposals — of the responsible and the irresponsible — the practicable and the impracticable — the advantageous and the disadvantageous — the right and the wrong.

We do not deny to European Philanthropists and Christians that right of interference which we have claimed for ourselves — the right of Christian good-will, which is as wide as the world. "There is no evil on the face of the earth, which may not be rightly discussed, and for which just relief may not be attempted by any man on the face of the earth. Man to man, may speak for man, under no other restriction but to speak the words of truth, justice, and kindness, and no man or people has the right to gainsay." * We object only to the indiscriminate outcry, not to the benevolent intention. On the other hand, as it was our desire to engage in aid of the best measures of well-being our own Northern Philanthropy, so it is now, to engage that of Europe also to the same high purpose, both, as we believe, equally misdirected, to the injury of the very cause they profess to promote.

No doubt it is too much to assume that the Remedial Code proposed is absolutely perfect. Yet, with all readiness to question the details, we have the

* Page 47.

utmost confidence in the great principle on which it proceeds, *of meeting an existing fact as a fact, and not as a proposal,* and therefore of turning the question from abolition to well-being, from the irresponsible to the responsible; of breaking only the bad bonds and retaining the good, both of master and slave, until, the word slavery remaining or disappearing, the whole condition of Africa in America shall be such as is due to a Christian country and a Christian age. We do not propose to the responsible States to omit any duty to which a true Christian philanthropy calls — to cancel in regard to slavery one jot or tittle of the golden rule. Whatever ills attach to the African or the European race in point of fact, this work adopts them no more for the one than for the other; and requires equally for both all possible reliefs and benefits. It is not therefore to justify any wrong, to apologize for any removable evil, that this work is now offered to the consideration of our European advisers, but to engage their co-operation and influence in the work of good will to man required by the actual facts of African slavery in the United States. To this end we submit some introductory illustrations — suited, as we think, to correct their mistaken views.

1. One error of our foreign friends consists in addressing their Appeals to the citizens of the United States, as if in their National capacity, they were responsible for slavery in the several slave-holding States, in any other than the general sense, in which the Appellants themselves are responsible for the social conditions of the several European Nations, or

even for American slavery itself. We ask their careful attention to the argument,* showing who are, in the matter of slavery, ordained of God as the " Powers that be." Surely they must see that, by the ordinance of Heaven, the authority in all matters existing in 1776, and not transferred to the *United* States, *is* with each separate State ; precisely as the authority of Great Britain, France, Austria, Prussia, or Russia, is over the social conditions of *each* of those nations, and not in any Congress of nations, whether temporary and special, or fixed and permanent like the American Union. No majorities in the august assemblies of such a Congress would have authority from HIM by whom " kings reign and princes decree justice," to abolish the serfdom of Russia, to restore the lost rights of the French Noblesse, to divide the domains of the Landholders of Great Britain, and to equalize the whole social condition of the high and the low in Austria and Prussia. These matters belong, by the ordinance of Heaven, to each several nation for itself ; each has its own separate authority and responsibility. Any appeal in regard to them must be made to each by itself, and not to the whole as a Congress of Nations. In like manner the United States are not to be appealed to in regard to the social condition of the several States existing when their Union was formed. The general interests, which their common language and peculiar circumstances and an overruling Providence have enabled them to unite, giving them some advantage over adjacent European States

* Chapters VII. — XII.

do not destroy the limits by which God, for wise purposes, made them separate; give them no authority over the original and inherent right of each separate sovereignty.

Besides — if there were the authority of the whole over the parts in the matter in question — there is lacking the power by which alone authority can have vitality. If, as we have asserted and shown,* an overruling Providence has made an equilibrium between the slave-holding and the free States — if any supposable Northern majorities are counterbalanced by some compensatory powers of Southern minorities, then, any original authority would become nugatory by means of equibalanced forces, and all vital authority would cease. Equity itself can give no authority to equibalanced impotence; — can impose no duty.

Of this principle, take the most marked of European instances; Great Britain and France. — Is either responsible for the social condition of the other? Has either received from the Ruler of nations authority over the other; or, if the authority were claimed has either the power to overrule the other? In matters of essential equity has either the might, which alone could give the right, to overthrow the social conditions of the other? In such a warfare, can either acquire the responsibility of conquest; — the right and the duty of the stronger? Let centuries of war and blood answer the question which, in regard to its own relations, it behooves the New

---

* Chapter **X.**

World to answer by anticipation — before rival sections become " natural enemies," from generation to generation. Centuries of blood have given proof to all nations and all time, that God constituted Great Britain and France, two and not one, with no rightful authority and no overruling power in either. The Norman conquerors of England became successful only by the wisdom of forgetting France and becoming English. " The Kings of Great Britain, France, and Ireland," despite the claims and gifts and wars of generations, possessed but the empty title, could neither rule nor overrule the kingdom whose name they claimed. The strength which God gave them to rule their own fair domain, proved itself only impotence in the vain attempt to rule the neighboring kingdom, which God had made equal to themselves. Surely Great Britain is not to be appealed to, to abolish any social conditions of France, nor France, to abolish any social conditions of Great Britain, for God has given to neither nation, authority and power to rule and overrule the other — has not given the " might " which could make the " right," though the equity of the change were as clear as the noon-day.

With some differences indeed, but for reasons substantially similar, i. e., for lack of original authority and for equibalanced impotence, the Northern States are not to be appealed to in the matter of Southern slavery, neither in the National Congress, nor in any other way. Whatever may be the error of the South — God has given to the North neither authority nor power — has left them no other method but that of wise and friendly counsel. Impotence is not responsible for the acts of power. The palsied arm has **no** duties.

2. A second mistake of our Foreign Advisers is, the demand for the abolition of slavery on the ground of political consistency, in view of the Declaration of Independence and the Constitution of the United States. If we had National authority and power, does political consistency require it ? In answer to this question, let us seek for European illustration.

Let then the Documents of English liberty be compared — the true sources and patterns of our own. Did they require, — did they furnish equal immunities for all classes of the people, homogeneous though they were, without regard to actual conditions, to the forms and arrangements which years and ages previous had introduced and established ? Did Magna Charta, did the Bill of Rights, equalize all orders and ranks of men ? Let these documents be considered.

Magna Charta, then, reclaimed the ancient rights of the Barons of England against the encroachments of the Crown ; — no doubt enabling and requiring them to promote the well-being of their serfs, then the largest class, the great mass of the people ; but neither enabling nor requiring them to abolish serfdom and make their serfs politically and personally free, to the injury of both. The *Bill of Rights* reclaimed the ancient rights of the Lords and Commons of England against new encroachments of the Crown, in like manner enabling and requiring all practicable advantages for all classes of the people, but neither enabling nor requiring equal suffrage to the entire mass without distinction ; — left unchanged the existing franchises and those relations of property and labor which doomed the mass to the actual condition of "the poor," without a voice in the government of their country. It was never claimed that Magna Charta and the Bill of Rights equalized all classes of society actually existing at their date. *These documents went as far as they went and no farther,* and left all matters unnamed, to the slow progress of just principles in promoting the well-being of all orders of the people. No doubt there has been wrong in not using the powers reclaimed for the well-being of the laboring and struggling masses, but it was never intended by these documents that all conditions of society should have *one* rule and *one* measure of civil liberty. In the language of Macaulay with regard to the Bill of Rights, "They made nothing law, which had not been law before. . . . Their object was to make the restoration of a tyrant impossible, and to place upon the throne sovereigns under whom law and liberty might be secure "* with all practicable advantages for all conditions of men.

In like manner, the Documents of the American Revolution — the Declaration of Independence and the Constitution of the United States, *went as far as they went and no farther, did what they did and no more ;* reclaimed English principles for English men, and not for the native Indians, or the Africans settled in the land, neither of whom had any such principles to reclaim, or were prepared to receive and enjoy the

---

* Vol. ii. 2, 580, 615.

freedom of an English people; though the ruling quality assumed in those documents by the United "Englands" of America required from each all possible provision for every condition of people in any way under their government, whether to regulate their freedom or to ameliorate their slavery. These American documents "made nothing law which was not law before;" and the American Revolution stands precisely in the same relation to existing facts, as do the two great eras of British liberty — making no immediate changes in the relation of any inhabitants of the land, and yet containing the elements, and therefore the obligation, of progressive improvement for all. At the time of the Declaration of Independence, slavery, like serfdom in Great Britain eight hundred years ago, existed in every state but one; and slaves remained slaves afterwards, precisely as serfs remained serfs after Magna Charta, and peasants, peasants after the Bill of Rights, with no change whatever, but yet with every claim to be *cared for* by each body politic, as kindness and justice might from time to time require.

If this view be thought inconsistent with the broad language of the Declaration of Independence, with the equal rights into which all men "are born," it needs only to consider the specifications of the Document itself, which are found, not to be the common rights of men, as men, but the rights of Englishmen as Englishmen — rights brought by the colonists from England, and existing by charter and custom, from the first. If the specifications are not as broad as the general expression, they necessarily limit and explain it; can in no way be extended by it to other people, and to other matters, than those which are specified. If there be a literal inconsistency, it cannot be helped, and must find its practical commendation and its just issue, not in admitting free Indians and enslaved Africans to the privileges of Englishmen, which would be no privileges to them, but in such use of the governing power as shall best promote the well-being of both. And in regard to it we may adopt the language of Macaulay concerning the resolution of Parliament which preceded and secured the Bill of Rights. "In fact, the one beauty of it was its inconsistency." Like that resolution, the Declaration stated and secured its great object, if not in perfect logical agreement with its general expression, yet in perfect consistency with any just view of its broadest terms. "Life, liberty, and the pursuit of happiness," to which all men are declared entitled, cannot be so understood as to interfere with either of the three. "Liberty" has "life" and "the pursuit of happiness" as its manifest and necessary limitations. The question remains with regard to all men that "are born," of all ages, sexes, classes, and conditions — *how much* liberty, in their actual case, does best promote and secure these primary and highest purposes. To be in any worthy sense equally free, that is, with reference to "life" and "the pursuit of happiness," the various classes and conditions of men must be *unequally free,* strange as the paradox may seem. In this sense, men and women, parents and children, masters and apprentices, in our own European population, *are* equally free. Who shall say that with slavery ameliorated — its bonds to labor and maintain labor retained, and its bad bonds removed — that Southern masters and their African slaves may not be equally free, that is, equally entitled to " life " and " the pursuit of happiness." When the government shall become truly patriarchal, at once in just regulation and in paternal protection, it will prove the most perfect freedom.*

3. A third mistake of our Foreign Advisers consists in demanding for slavery, as an existing fact, the same refusal as for the proposal to enslave.

No mistake is more plain. Every where and always, we must refuse the proposal to change the condition of our fellow-men from the better to the worse; but this does not require, for it does not enable us to change instantly and absolutely the worse for the better, to annihilate any or all distinctions on a scale of endless variety. Poverty, sickness, wounds, are in this respect in the same category as slavery. We may accept no proposal to inflict them, but this does not require, for it does not enable us to abolish them. All that is required, in either case, is to meet the actual condition with all kindness and justice, to alleviate all evils, and bestow all benefits, to our utmost power. We must refuse utterly and instantly the proposal to engage in highway robbery; but we are not therefore required to restore utterly and instantly the " man wounded and half dead " to soundness and his goods, but only to dress his wounds, provide for his wants, and aid his recovery according to our

* Compare pp. 133, 134.

power.   The divine illustration of love to our neighbor requires no more.

The impossibility of treating facts, like the proposal to introduce them, lies, in the very nature of things, in the arrangements of the world — embracing toils, exposures, sufferings, of exceeding inequality from the very heights of wealth down to the deepest extremes of poverty and woe.   In sober truth, it is not man but God, it is not human will but the ordinance of Heaven, which makes it the necessity of every country, and of every age, that existing conditions should be incapable of instant and absolute abolition — should admit only of alleviation and improvement.   The necessity is for substance the same in Europe and America.   *The labor must be done* at once for the livelihood of the laborers themselves — their employers and mankind, or all must suffer a severer doom than labor and exposure in any form which has ever been endured.   The mightiest governments of earth have their limits; are not competent to remove social evils, nay, even social abuses, at their will; are restrained to the one work within their power, of gradual amelioration — none the less where the mass of the people are nominally free, none the more where they are enslaved.   We proceed to name European instances, neither for reproach nor self-justification, but to make plain the principles which must govern Europe and America alike in dealing with great social facts, with existing conditions of society.

Take first the *mining* of Europe, with all its exposures and miseries — the work on which all other work depends, the labor by which all other labor is alleviated and aided, at once the severest and the most indispensable of the occupations of mankind; without which there can be no provision for multitudes of men, no ease and comfort of civilized life. *Mining* is an existing fact, an actual institution, dooming a few, compared with the whole race benefited by it, and yet thousands, to the severest labors, exposures, and sufferings, and incidentally but actually, to abuses which call for relief. And yet, it cannot be instantly and absolutely abolished, without greater evils even to the miners themselves, without damage to the whole well-being of the race, without dooming the world to a ruin worse than all the toils, exposures, sufferings, and even abuses of the mines. You cannot abolish the miner's lot, unless you can abolish God's ordinance when he built the earth and hid in its depths the treasures of iron and coal, and silver and gold, for the use of countless millions of men, — to ennoble and alleviate their labors, — to limit and lessen their exposures and sufferings, to provide more abundantly for their wants. You can no more abolish mining and the miner's lot, than you can level the mountains and raise the depths in which the stores of ages have been gathered by the hand of the Almighty — than you can command to the surface the whole material for the instruments with which the earth is tilled, and its productions wrought for the food, and raiment, and comfort of mankind, and for the very coin by which what is thus provided is distributed to the families of all nations. All you can do is to ameliorate the indispensable lot — to remove as far and as fast as possible its manifest abuses — to make it as easy, as safe, as advantageous to the actual miners as the indispensable labor permits — leaving only the toil, exposure, and suffering essential to the lot which God's wise providence has ordered. The steam engine, and the safety lamp, and the attempts of the British Parliament to correct abuses which fill the mind with horror, all indicate the amelioration which is possible, and not the abolition which is impossible. The miners must still be left to their lot, in the assurance that nothing which Heaven has arranged is without its mercy and its lesson, without the axiom made plain to every mind of man and taught in every lot — to prosperity in its greatest heights, to poverty in its lowest depths, to the miners even, in the bowels of the earth. "Surely," says the most ancient of all books, "there is a vein for the silver, and a place for gold, where they fine it. Iron is taken out of the earth, and brass is molten out of the stone. . . . There is a path which no fowl knoweth, and which the vulture's eye hath not seen. He putteth forth his hand upon the rock; he overturneth the mountains by the roots. He cutteth out rivers among the rocks, and his eye seeth every precious thing; he bindeth the floods from overflowing; and the thing that is hid bringeth he forth to light. But where shall wisdom be found? and where is the place of understanding? . . . And unto man he said, Behold the fear of the Lord, that is wisdom; and to depart from evil is understanding."* When

* Job xxviii.

God made it needful that the replenished earth should live by mining, he did not bury the miners beneath his highest mercy, the best boon of life; beneath the reach of all the beatitudes.

The same necessity — the same paradox of toil, exposure, and suffering in order to the greatest ease, safety, and enjoyment — the same irreversible doom of some, at once for their own benefit and the benefit of all — the same liability to abuse, and the same moral opportunity, — belong to the great mass of mankind, occupied in the labors by which men live, and for which mining provides the indispensable material; — the same impossibility of immediate and absolute abolition, and even of the abuses at any time actual, but not essential to the doom. There can be no immediate and absolute abolition of the condition of the laboring classes of Europe — of "the poor," the "lower classes," the "peasantry," the "operatives" — at the best, dependent on scanty wages, and at the worst, "suffering masses" outnumbering the means of employment and support. This condition of the laborers of Europe is an existing fact, to be met in all kindness and justice by individuals and governments, as a fact to be regarded, — but not as a proposal to be instantly and absolutely rejected. Parliaments, Kings, Emperors cannot turn great national facts into non-existence — cannot put them into mere proposals — can no more emancipate "the poor," the "lower classes," the "peasantry," the "operatives," the "serfs," of their several governments, than they can emancipate the miners from their lot, — than they can emancipate the human race from the use of iron, and coal, and silver, and gold, and food, and raiment, and house, and home. All they can do, is by all the means in their power to alleviate the miseries and correct the abuses of every lot.

Suppose it assumed on our side the Atlantic, that the system of small farming and a working yeomanry in our Northern States, is the true idea of social well-being, and that we require all Europe to adopt it — instantly and absolutely to emancipate " the poor," to raise to social equality " the lower classes," to abolish the poverty of " the masses," to divide the wide domains of unenlightened ages, and establish every where laborers on their little farms after the manner of New England.

Vain and absurd demand! as impossible as to remove the mountains! If it were a proposal to bring the New England yeomanry into the condition of the European " poor," there would be reason and conscience in rejecting it. If Europe had the power, it would have no right to force upon us the undesirable change, to rob us of our birthright enjoyment — of the gift of Providence inherited from our fathers. But it is quite another thing to undertake the impossibility of putting *their* masses into our condition — of changing the doom which Providence has imposed as the inheritance from many generations. What God has permitted to grow for ages, man has no power to change in a day. He may reject the proposal to plant the seed, but he cannot uproot the stern growth of centuries.

Vain and absurd demand! The very pattern we propose for Europe to follow, only illustrates the impossibility of following it. How came that condition of the laboring masses in America which is proposed as a pattern to the greater masses of Europe ? Came it at the instant, at the call of man or by the decree of any government on earth, that you should require Sovereigns and Parliaments to " charm " it into being ? Rather, did it not require a new world for the theatre of a minute experiment, and the slow emigration of a medium class, " the siftings of three kingdoms," and then the time of two centuries, to establish governments, create habits, and form communities capable of assimilating and absorbing *moderate* proportions of the European peasantry ? The governments of New England, New York, Pennsylvania, the models of the North, could not have been instituted *at all*, by the crowds of European peasants now thronging our shores. If their emigration had been rapid at first, the New England condition of a working yeomanry would never have existed on our continent, nor been capable of its present work of assimilation and absorption. Even now, there are complaints that they come too fast, whether for their advantage or our own. What else means our " Americanism," our objection to the ingress of these hundreds of thousands every year, but our dread of a too rapid increase of the European " lower classes ; " — but our acknowledgment, that a population homogeneous with ourselves cannot come instantly into the full inheritance of the lot which the providence of two hundred years has given us ; that Europe cannot change by decree the condition of the masses of her people ; must leave them to their inherited doom, with only those alleviations and benefits which kindness and justness can bestow — those progressive improvements of which they can only plant the seed and cherish the growth.

The impossibility of annihilating great social facts, as the proposal to introduce them might be rejected, applies equally to the most despotic and to the most republican of the European Powers. The Russian Autocrat and the British Parliament are alike impotent to change the existing conditions of the masses of their people. The nobility and the serfs of the one, the aristocracy and peasantry, with the middle classes, of the other, exist in fixed relations of poverty and wealth, neither at the bidding nor the forbidding of " the powers that be." The Parliament, were it ever so much inclined to benefit the whole people — to bless the masses — the Autocrat, with whatever wisdom and good will — have their necessary limit — are precluded by the circumstances actually existing, by the rooted strength of ages, from instant and absolute change. There is no power in governments, despotic or free, to enrich " the poor," to raise " the lower classes," to banish the " misery of the masses," to emancipate " the serfs," to change the condition of European laborers into that of the working yeomanry of New England, as there is to reject any proposal to bring the working yeomanry of these States into the condition of European serfs and peasants. All that can be done, and all that is required, is, according to the abilities of the several governments, and the capabilities of the several people, to bestow such reliefs and benefits as are possible in the conditions actually existing — such as are continually attempted by the British Parliament for England, Scotland, and Wales, and even for Ireland itself, only with a wisdom and kindness never to pause until the utmost limits of well-being have been reached. The Russian Autocrat can do no more — will find himself hindered or baffled in his endeavors, if in his desire for rapid improvement, he transcends the bounds which conditions, established by ages, have made as firm as the mountains. These bounds he may or may not have sufficiently regarded, in providing for the freedom of serfs homogeneous with the higher classes of society. Time alone can settle the question whether he have retained duly the bonds which make free, and duly rejected the freedom which enslaves. There are limits, on the one side and on the other, to the proposals of the Czar. Some bonds are retained upon both masters and serfs, no doubt designed to prevent in Russia the great evil of Southern Europe — of masses " miserably free." In Russia, now, as in all the world and in all time, then only can beneficial changes be wrought in long established conditions of society, when mutual relations and obligations are duly regarded, in view of the whole past conditions of the people; then only can the well-being of its serfs be duly provided for, when the mutual dependence of property and labor is duly regarded, when bad bonds are progressively broken, and good bonds retained and strengthened. The nineteenth century's civilization, Christianity, instead of requiring, forbid the immediate and absolute abolition of Russian serfdom — instead of forbidding, require some bonds retained upon the existing and long established property of the country; and if so, some bonds on the existing and long established labor of the country also, that property may be able to fulfil its obligations; — while at the same time, there is forbidden every abuse and required every possible amelioration and advantage for the whole people, whether bond or free.

The impossibility of immediate and absolute change in actual social conditions, even in homogeneous Europe, has always existed. The Europe that now calls upon America to treat the fact of African slavery like the proposal to enslave, has given proof for ages, that it asks an impossibility. In truth, the existing conditions of any period of its history, as they were never due to the governments of that period, but to previous acts and methods which gave them their prevalence, so they were out of the power of cotemporary authority, except by such corrections and ameliorations as might grow at length into beneficial substitutes. European serfdom was not the infliction of the lords of the soil, paramount at any period, but the growth of ages; partly from the original barbarian condition, partly by conquest and oppression, and partly by methods of relief and security to which various exposures gave rise. Originating with the barbarism of the European nations, the low condition of the masses might have proved worse, might have continued longer, if feudalism had not intervened with its protecting, governing, and providing care, as well as its oppression.*   The barbarian starting-points, and the element

---

* Guizot, vol. iii. pp. 122, 123.

of conquest and subjugation, are older than Julius Cæsar who describes them; — even Great Britain having been visited by continental conquerors and settlers, before the Roman, the Saxon, the Danish, and the Norman invasions, by which its enserfed condition became extended and established — at every point, beyond the removal of any cotemporary governments.

The impossibility thus due to long established social conditions and belonging to European serfdom, explains the chasm of history in regard to its abolition. *There is no history, because there could be none.* No direct, positive, absolute and general emancipation was ever made by any decree or succession of decrees of which history could make record; — the emancipation, such as it was, being every where only casual and incidental, the growth of time and circumstance, the only method possible of changing the condition of the masses of the people in all countries and all times.

Indeed, whatever condemnation may be due to those warlike tribes, the Franks, the Saxons and the Normans, who conquered and enserfed the European masses, when each new step of serfdom was a proposal capable of being refused; — whether a condition advancing by conquest and oppression be regarded as an unmixed evil, or as a providential method of evolving modern industry and civilization from the indolence and improvidence of savage life; — *after the deed was done,* and established relations and conditions existed, there was no power in European monarchs or lords to abolish the actual institution —

to do more than to correct and ameliorate up to the just relations of property and labor. "No great fact, no social state makes its appearance complete and at once."* "The change, great as it was, (in Great Britain,) was the effect of gradual development, not of demolition and reconstruction. The exorbitant power of the Barons was gradually reduced, the condition of the peasants gradually elevated. . . . That revolution which put an end to property in man, was silently and imperceptibly effected."† "The evil was mingled with the institutions of the country, and required much time and successive efforts for its eradication."‡

The impossibility of immediate and absolute change is still more manifest in the issues of even this slow emancipation, — silently and imperceptibly effected, as alone was possible, making it a caution and not a pattern, and requiring in all future attempts some new method not included in the received idea of emancipation and freedom. There is manifest enough (on which we have dwelt §) "the misery of the masses," indicating that in the slow progress from serfdom there was not a sufficient reservation of mutual bonds; and there *were*, certainly, for many ages, extreme social difficulties and disorders, due undoubtedly, in degree, to the premature and indiscreet emancipation of lords and serfs — to "too free a freedom." The just view forced itself upon the mind of Puffendorf, more than a century ago, in view of evils

---

* Guizot, vol. iii. p. 17.   † Macaulay, vol. i. pp. 21, 23.

‡ A History of the Poor Law, by Sir George Nicholas, Secretary of the Poor Law Board.

§ See Chapter VI. "European Experiments with Serfdom."

of which there is history enough. " To be held within the limits of slavery which the natural law of support prescribes, apart from the cruelty of some masters and the rigor of certain laws, — in this, there is no undue severity. For this compulsory subjection is compensated by the advantage of being assured of a livelihood, whilst hired laborers know not often how to subsist, whether for want of being hired or their own laziness, which cannot be cured without blows. This laziness men have endeavored to remedy, by the establishment of workhouses, a sort of prison, to make men work, whether they will or no. Some have thought, not without reason, that the prohibition of slavery among Christian nations, hath chiefly occasioned that flood of thieving vagrants and sturdy beggars which is usually complained of."* The same view forces itself upon those who are occupied at the present day in the endeavor to remedy the consequences of ancient mistakes by new legislation. Sir George Nicholas, in his elaborate history of the poor laws, says: " The change from a state of slavery was attended with a certain amount of evil — led to a great increase of vagrancy. That there was cause for coercive legislation, cannot be denied." He accordingly refers to the laws of centuries to compel labor and to supply the wants of the poor — from Edward II. to Elizabeth, ending in those famous poor laws, rendered necessary by the condition of society, and intended to be equally binding upon property and labor, of the one-sided application of which Black-

---

* Puffendorf, Book VI. chap. iii. sec. 10.

stone complains.* However lacking history is in regard to emancipation from serfdom, there is no lack of record of the fearful condition of society which was the consequence, when the police and provision of serfdom ceased to be compulsory on property and labor, and the only remedy men saw was a partial restoration of the bonds prematurely broken. Surely the abolition of serfdom in Europe, though slow enough, was premature and indiscreet, and is not an example to be followed, but a caution to be carefully regarded; requiring, wherever slavery is found, all just bonds retained both on property and labor, — some indispensable coercion upon both, in order that the functions of both may be duly performed; — preventing the idleness and improvidence which a premature freedom might give to the laborer, and the parsimony and neglect which a premature freedom might give to the employer; — taking beforehand the same liberty which in every land the most free nations are compelled to take — in requiring property to support the poor, and the poor to work according to their ability.

These European instances illustrate the principles applicable to both continents alike, and are only the more imperative in America on account of wide differences in civilization and race. If actual conditions of men essentially homogeneous cannot be instantly and absolutely abolished, and when abolished by slow degrees and unobserved processes, have furnished instances of warning and caution instead of encourage-

* See " Slavery and the Remedy," p. 39.

ment, how doubly impossible the work, when the ruling and the subject races have such remarkable differences ; — the African not only lower in the social scale by direct inheritance from barbarian ancestors, but marked by physical characteristics, which always distinguish him. No European successes could decide in favor of the immediate and absolute emancipation of African slaves and American masters. How much more is the example withdrawn, and a double impossibility assured by European *ill* success, even with a homogeneous people and emancipation by slow degrees. Vagabondage and violence requiring law, and law, failing to recover from vagabondage and violence — wide-spread pauperism requiring relief, and all measures of relief failing to provide for that wide-spread pauperism — centuries passed, and still showing "miserable masses," which baffle the wisest legislation and philanthropy, where the people are essentially of one blood — these results of European emancipation, all-pervading, long-enduring, and, to all human view, irretrievable, — how distinctly and solemnly do they forewarn the greater difficulty, the more absolute impossibility in the matter of African slavery in America, — opening to the view a " misery of the masses" of which homogeneous Europe cannot furnish a type.*

---

* In requiring an ameliorated slavery, instead of instant and absolute freedom for the benefit of the African race, as lower in the social scale, we abstain, as in the work itself, from any assertion of their natural inferiority, as entirely irrelevant to the question ; — assured that the rights of one race over another have not been submitted to their own judgment of superiority ; that no claim to be " the Celestial Empire " can give Heaven's authority, either to enslave or hold in slavery any portion of mankind. We simply take the facts

XXX

The difficulties belonging to differences of civilization and race are abundantly set forth in the original work,* and in the subsequent Review of the Decision of the Supreme Court in the case of Dred Scott. There are intrinsic difficulties — there may be also unreasonable prejudice; but both unite in the argument *against* immediate and absolute emancipation, for something better than immediate and absolute freedom. "The laws which have been passed and enforced by the States most exposed to large proportions of free African population, and the reasons given for those laws, show most plainly, that there is not 'free soil' for the freed African in all our wide America. With the minutest exceptions, in every town, and county, and state, North as well as South, every body thinks that the African race, improved though they have been, since their emigration, are not entitled to be, in large numbers, part and parcel with the Anglo-Saxon race — to be advantageously to themselves or the whole people, parts of the several 'Englands' of the new world."

as they are, without deciding how they might have been, if the circumstances of the two races had been interchanged, or how they may become hereafter. It is enough for our argument, that the African *is* less advanced in civilization and its adjuncts, even though admitted equally capable of advancement, and his actual inferiority were referred entirely to the providential arrangement, which fixed his place of habitation on the earth. Dare the European race proudly say, that if God had assigned *them* their place behind the great African Desert and in the depths of the torrid zone, and had given temperate Europe to the Negro, with its gulfs, and bays, and rivers, for the easy communication of civilization and Christianity from their great centres, that the Negro of the nineteenth century would not have been the superior, in all that can exalt and bless mankind? Whatever might or might not have been, — the barbarism of Central Africa is an actual fact, has been only partially removed from the race in the United States, and must be taken into the account in any proposals for their well-being.

* Pages 21, 80, and 129 — 132.

If any thing be wanted to intensify the argument from the differences of civilization and race, it may be had in the words of the great champion* of free soil, in his speech on Kansas, in the Senate of the United States, March 3, 1858. "Free labor," says the Senator, "has at last apprehended its rights, its interests, its powers, its destiny, and is organizing itself to assume the government of the Republic. It will meet you every where, in the Territories and out of them, wherever you may go to extend slavery: It has driven you back in California and Kansas. It will invade you soon in Delaware, Maryland, Virginia, Missouri, and Texas. It will meet you in Arizona, in Central America, and even in Cuba. You may, indeed, get a start under or near the Tropics, but it will be for a short time. Even there, you will found states for free labor to maintain and occupy." . . . "The interests of the white race demand the ultimate emancipation of all men. The white man needs this continent to labor on. His head is clear, his arm is strong, and his necessities are fixed. *He must and will have it*." Alas, how extremes meet! The highest philanthropy and the deepest cruelty are at one! The demand is for freedom for the African race, and yet they are not to have room for the sole of their foot!— there is to be no "free soil for the freed African in all our wide America"! Surely, there is an overruling Providence which turns men's counsels against themselves, and makes them to establish what they intended to destroy. There is no argument so

* Hon. W. H. Seward.

intense against immediate and absolute abolition, and in favor of an ameliorated and protecting slavery, as is furnished by the expressions and practices of the advocates of free soil in the United States.

The conclusion from European instances — more decisive in view of differences of race — is required by the whole history of mankind; an immediate and absolute abolition of a great social institution has never occurred since the world began : — rather, *never but once*, and then, under such conditions as make the impossibility only the more plain, when it is proposed as the mere work of man under the common providence of God : *once, and once only ;* — the exception proving the rule, by which the most powerful nations must needs govern themselves in their undertakings for the masses of their people. It was only by the strong hand and outstretched arm of the Almighty, over-ruling the universal laws which govern human things, that the threefold impossibility was accomplished in favor of the tribes of Israel instantly and absolutely released from Egyptian bondage. *Miracles* from heaven delivered them from the power which held them in slavery — *miracles* opened their path through the sea, and fed, and clothed, and governed, and taught, and disciplined them, forty years in the wilderness, until a new generation was prepared for settlement in the promised land : and *miracles* prepared for them their final habitation, giving them houses which they builded not, wells which they digged not, and fields which they planted not : — the whole, most manifestly, withdrawing their example, unless the same commands, the same signs and wonders require again what is utterly impossible, and therefore not required, under the common providence of God. The whole history of mankind, with this single exception, itself joining the testimony, confirms our conclusion from general principles and European experiments, that immediate and absolute emancipation is impossible, and must be doubly impossible in the case of African slavery in the United States.

———————

This confident assurance has not been adopted without considering the example of the British West Indies, concerning which claims so opposite are urged. Instead of attempting to decide upon conflicting testimony, we have preferred to admit in degree the most favorable accounts, and to maintain the alleged impossibility notwithstanding. Admitting, then, all that is claimed by the most sanguine friends of emancipation in the West Indies, we assert that its success is neither so assured nor so complete as to make it an example for the United States if the cases were alike; while they are plainly so unlike, that the restricted and regulated emancipation in the one, if the success were assured and complete, would require restrictions and regulations in the other suited to the case, and in our belief, the ameliorated slavery which this work proposes.

1. The success of West India emancipation is neither so assured nor so complete as to make it an example. It is plainly too early in its history

to give assurance of success. The Bishop of **Bar**-badoes, expecting final success, admits that there are many evils, but claims that two or even three gener-ations are needful, before the ill effects of slavery can be entirely removed, and the success of emancipation be complete.* Be it so. But then, also, it is equally right to say, that two or three generations must pass before the *good* effects of slavery can be lost, and the *ill* success of the emancipation be complete. In truth, a longer time is required before either the good or the evil issues can be decided by experience. Though there were at the end of twenty years no occasion for misgiving in regard to those whose habits of life, and relations to property and skill, were so suddenly changed, a longer trial would be needful to determine the question. Much more, when there are acknowledged evils as well as hopeful appearances, it must be impossible to decide whether the one or the other be due to the slavery abolished or to the free-dom bestowed. If the evils remaining may be re-ferred to the influences of slavery, which it requires two or three generations to remove, then may any hopeful appearances be referred to the influences of slavery not yet entirely vanished away. The old habits of labor on the one hand, and of capital and arrangement on the other, may not yet have lost their force, and there may be remaining some of the advantages of a regular and regulated industry — of due labor and maintenance, preventing the evils of "too free a freedom," but giving no assurance

* Letter dated Feb. 23, 1858, in National Era, Aug. 12.

of a favorable issue when that force is lost. The
"train" does not instantly stop when the "power" is
removed, but goes forward almost as before. Nevertheless, gravitation and friction are producing their
gradual effect, and the whole force will be expended
at last. Admit all the favorable appearances claimed,
and they give no absolute assurance of a successful
emancipation.

Besides the uncertainty of the final issues, the success at its present stage is manifestly too incomplete
to make a decisive example. Difficulties and evils
are admitted which break the charm, and throw us
back upon general principles and the whole experience of mankind. Such admissions as those of the
Bishop of Barbadoes and others, with regard to Barbadoes and the smaller islands where the circumstances are peculiarly favorable, give ground for the
assertion that even in them the success is too incomplete to become our example. Much more do the
larger islands, as we understand the admissions of the
friends of emancipation, give this ground, in greater
degrees of idleness, improvidence, and vagrancy, fore-
warning the evils which prevailed in Europe for centuries, and have issued in the "miserable masses" of
the nineteenth century, with whatever enhancement
differences of race and climate may produce.

That the success of West India emancipation is
thus incomplete, is confirmed by certain important
facts which admit of no other explanation. How
else can we explain the act of the Legislature of
Jamaica, meeting idleness and vagrancy with such
provisions as to be objected to by Lord Brougham,

in the House of Lords, as "reducing the free negro population to slavery."* Laws are provided for occasions, which, however exaggerated, can never be entirely non-existent. There must be idleness and vagrancy, with the fear of their increase, or such a law could never have been proposed.

The actual evils and the dreaded danger are implied, also, in the methods of emancipation proposed by other European governments having tropical possessions, viz., the retaining some good bonds, instead of loosing all, in order that the evils and dangers of the British West Indies may be avoided. Thus, the Dutch ordinance for liberating fifty thousand slaves in Surinam, *retains bonds*, instead of making emancipation complete. Says the Kingston Journal, " Upon being liberated, the slaves are not to be left unconditionally to their own control, and the control of those who are ready to take advantage of their ignorance to impose upon them, as in this and the other British colonies. At the same time, the former slave-holders are protected against the evils arising from the want of labor, as the emancipated will not become the unrestricted owners of their own time and labor. The duties they are to perform are to be made known by general orders, but all slaves who shall repay to the government the amount paid for their freedom, are to be exempt from these orders. Another, and by far one of the most wholesome provisions in the law, is that all who obtain their freedom are to contribute on fixed terms towards a fund for

* London Morning Chronicle, March 23, 1848.

repaying the government the cost of their freedom — also for religious teaching, education of children, nursing of the sick and relief of the poor and aged. With us in the West Indies, the absence of such regulations at the general emancipation, involved us in difficulties, against which at the present time we have to fight a hard battle."

The Danish method at Santa Cruz indicates a like caution — requiring, as we understand, an "annual affiliation" — the only freedom being the power of changing masters and service, without the liberty to have no master, or to strike for higher wages.

It does not answer the argument to ascribe the evils acknowledged to the proprietors and not to the laborers — to the emancipated masters and not to the emancipated slaves. It only gives prominence to the necessity of bonds upon property, that labor may have due opportunity and provision, while it requires, of course, corresponding bonds on labor, without which bonds on property would be of no avail. If the emancipated masters have used their freedom unjustly towards the native-born laborers, *they* were made too free, and should have remained under some of their former bonds. But then, of necessity, the slaves also were made too free, and should have remained under such bonds as would enable the masters to fulfil their obligations.

Neither does it answer the argument to produce instances of African advancement in property and station; for the all-important question is, the effect upon the mass, and not upon excepted cases. Besides, a just amelioration could not fail to secure *more* excepted cases without the evils resulting from the whole system of labor and provision abolished. The "misery of the masses" in England is not less deplorable, because out of "the poor," "the peasantry," "the operatives," individuals sometimes rise to wealth and rank. In this case also, wiser measures for the masses would no doubt have resulted in more instances of individual advancement, without the evil of wide-spread wretchedness.

2. But the two cases are plainly *unlike*, — emancipation in the West Indies, being with bonds remaining and imposed, impossible in the United States, and requiring some corresponding bonds suited to our different condition. Let the actual bonds of the emancipated colonies be briefly stated and duly compared.

There is then, first, the physicial condition and relations. The insular position itself, and in the islands where the success is most confidently affirmed, the narrow limits, render labor still dependent upon property, and property still dependent upon labor, as before emancipation, — are bonds upon both, impossible in our continental position. The climate also — within the Tropics — protects African labor from European competition, obliges the property in the soil to employ the laborers born upon the soil, and protects them from the " clear head and strong arm and fixed necessities " and determined will of the white man : again, an impossible bond even at our remotest South — and more and more impossible as we approach the North.

There is, next, the political condition of the emancipated colonies : — the British government — direct, positive, powerful, prompt, in its colonial administration — with its actual and visible array, inspiring a sense of unavailing resistance and impossible escape — the " arcanum of empire " — always ready to exert its reserved power — acting when it does not act — vigorous when inert — governing when it does not govern, by its prestige of promptness and efficiency.

And this prompt and efficient government has no need to await the consent of the governed mass, unqualified and new to the work of self-government — to await the making or the executing of the laws by which they may be directed or restrained, as must be the case with us if the freed slaves are admitted to equal privileges with the white race, — to our universal suffrage. The property or rental which makes a voter in the British West Indies excludes the mass of freed negroes, and leaves them therefore under the bonds of law and police which the property of the country — the minority of the whole people — may see fit to retain or renew, subject only to that royal authority and power which gives efficiency to their own. Surely there are needful with us some corresponding bonds suited to the fact of universal suffrage.

Moreover, this prompt and efficient government, unhindered in its action, has more than its own inherent potency and prestige — it has actual direction and restraint, *special regulations and provisions*, new bonds in place of old bonds loosed, to be enforced if need be, with its whole array of power, and therefore not likely to need enforcement. Thus, in Antigua, says the Superintendent of Police, " The numerical force of this district is eleven sergeants and two officers. Five of these sergeants are on duty every twenty-four hours. One remains in charge of the premises, *arms*, and stores. Four patrol night and day, and have also to attend to the duties of the magistrate, and the other is employed by me in general patrol duties, pointing out nuisances and irregularities. . . . . A due fear of, and prompt obedience to, the authority of the magistrates, is a prominent feature of the lower orders, and to this ['bond'] I attribute, mainly, the maintenance of rural tranquillity."* At Barbadoes, also, where emancipation is considered specially successful, there *is*, as reported by a resident there the very last winter, (1858,) "a large and most efficient Police, armed with clubs, and recognized by appropriate badges, with a signal post, by means of which the whole police force can be concentrated on any point, and if needful, sustained by the whole military force of the island. Surely the conclusion is just — insular position — climate — efficient and prompt government, and special regulations and provisions — are bonds — and if the 'quasi' emancipation were ever so successful, the example would require in our wide-spread continent, temperate climate, universal suffrage, an inefficient Police, some corresponding bonds — some 'quasi' slavery."

These are some of the reasons for our confident assurance from general principles and the whole course of history, that the absolute and immediate abo-

* Thorne & Kimball, pp. 44, 45.

lition of slavery in the United States is impossible —
the example of the British West Indies notwithstanding — that whatever refusal may be required on
any proposal to enslave anew, nothing can now be
done but with Christian kindness and wisdom, to retain those bonds upon property and labor, which are
manifestly for the well-being of the whole people, of
the African as well as the European race. The facts
of slavery are as real and as stubborn as the mountains, and are not to be brushed away as if they were
feathers. We can no more place the three millions
of African slaves in the condition of the Northern
yeomanry, or of the free whites at large, than we can
replace them in the savage wilds from which their
ancestors were torn; or, than we can do for them in
one year what Providence has done with ourselves in
two thousand of European and not African opportunity, and two hundred of cis-Atlantic discipline.
The question is not now whether we shall steal men
from Africa, and bring them through all the horrors
of the middle passage *into* slavery, but how shall we
meet the actual case of millions of slaves existing and
increasing in our land.

To this question there is but one just answer: At
whatever inconvenience the dominant race, individually and socially, must provide for the real well-being
of the millions committed to its charge, according to
its individual and social power, with equal good-will
to the African as the European race — none the less
to the African because he is enslaved; none the more
to the European because he is free.*

* Chapters IV. — VI.

d *

To this end of well-being is this work devoted. Allowing the proper essence of slavery, viz., the *being held to labor*, with the corresponding obligation to *maintain labor*, it requires that an existing institution, by which millions eat their bread and the wants of the race are provided for, shall not be abolished but retained ; while all the ills which are not of its essence shall be carefully and wisely mitigated or removed, and all advantages added which are possible in the actual case.

It is in aid of this high purpose, and not for base and wicked ends, that we have invoked a NEW ERA* in Northern as well as Southern opinion and effort, instead of the vain and useless struggle to limit and abolish on the one hand, or to perpetuate and extend on the other ;—a calm, deliberate, and persevering attempt to introduce "counsels and methods as acceptable to the South as to the North, and as advantageous to the African as the European race in their mysterious relations to each other."

It is with the same high purpose that we turn now from our own country to Europe, and invoke a NEW ERA in the opinions and counsels of our Foreign advisers : — not for evil, but for good — not for wrong, but for right; not for the oppression and ruin of the African race, but for their protection and advancement. We implore them not to encourage the vain struggle of equibalanced sections by appeals to the whole United States in a matter for which each separate State is alone responsible — not to require of America a political consistency of which Europe furnishes

* Page 120.

no example, and which is forbidden by the condition of the people to whom they claim its application;—and lastly, not to demand of the United States of America, with its incongenial races, an immediate and absolute change, which Europe never made with its peoples of one blood, and in the work of ages, failed of advantageous results; and that, instead, they will aid us in the only proper work for Christian philanthropists, joining that fellowship of impotence* to which we have called our Northern countrymen, as their mightiest power for African WELL–BEING:

* Page 74.

INTRODUCTION.

WE meet Slavery as a fact, not as a proposal. We have to do with slaveholding, not with slave-making. We seek not what should be done if there were no slaves, but what is right and best now that there are more than three millions. We seek the right method, and the best method in existing circumstances.

Admitting the evil of Slavery, and the imperious demand for a Remedial Code, but denying slaveholding as a crime *per se,* and immediate abolition as the remedy; — asserting that the African race is fixed, and must be provided for chiefly on our soil, and yet approving heartily colonization in Africa; — claiming that the climate and productions of the South, and the original and actual condition of the enslaved race, forbid the methods of the North and the Anglo-Saxon race; — turning the question from *mere* abolition and *mere* slavery, to the *well-being* of a people providentially on our hands; — and, lastly, fixing the responsibility upon each slaveholding State, separately, and denying it to the United States, — *a remedy is sought suited to the peculiar case,* — a REMEDIAL CODE, at least an experiment of relief and benefit, which wisely and successfully made by any single State, might lead the whole sisterhood in her train.

A Christian State, philanthropic, patriarchal, is bound to abolish just so much of Slavery as is injurious, and no more; to retain just so much as is beneficial, and no less. The Christian patriarch and Christian philanthropist need not be at variance, if they will but unite in the simple attempt to promote the well-being of the slaves in and with the well-being of the whole people.

The leading point to be kept in view in a Remedial Code, is to preserve the essential quality of Slavery without the evils which are not of its essence: in other words, to secure the two counterparts, the being "held to labor," and the being held to maintain labor, without the evils which now attach to both masters and slaves, and to the whole community directly or remotely connected. A Remedial Code must aim at the following purposes: —

1. To provide for the slaves, as a mass, something better than freedom; — such advantages and securities as shall compensate their being held to labor; so that a considerate slave might prefer the price of freedom, to freedom purchased by its price; and the whole mass of slaves have an interest in the continued institution.

2. To provide for the masters something better than "Slavery as it is;" a more available labor in return for the "rations" and privileges of the laborer; better service with less difficulties and fears: so that a considerate master might prefer the Remedial to the existing code; and the whole body of masters find their interest in aiding and sustaining it.

3. To provide for the free blacks and those becoming free something better than the present condition of their class; satisfactory to themselves, and at the same time harmless and helpful to the well-being of both masters and slaves.

4. Incidental, but of immeasurable importance, — to satisfy the conscience and philanthropy of the country, not merely by the "juste milieu," — the "happy medium" between evil extremes, — but to give full scope to the truest benevolence, the most

faithful duty, the most earnest Christian charity; in which the South, taking the indispensable lead, shall welcome with the whole heart the aid of the North.

The writer is deeply sensible of the difficulties in devising and executing such a code and with such results. But are there not greater difficulties in either other alternative?

If Slavery be retained "as it is," can it be without difficulties and woes, without fears and anxieties, which must despoil it of its essential quality of useful labor, of valuable service?

If Slavery be abolished, can it be without impracticable difficulties; whether at the South in providing for the well-being of both races in their new relations, or at the North when the tide of freed slaves shall come in like a flood.

But without comparison, such a code can be attempted and accomplished only in a Christian country and by a Christian people. To a Christian country and a Christian people, we make our appeal. The sense of responsibility, the benevolent intention, the reliance on infinite strength, must be supposed in order to the sincere attempt, and successful execution. But these supposed, then all difficulties are provided for, if the attempt be right and wise. . . . . If a Remedial Code be the true obedience to the golden rule; if Christian good will, if the love of our neighbor as ourselves, require not emancipation but amelioration, who shall dare discourage or forbid? Nothing is impossible with God. Nothing is impossible to him who believeth. No attempt within the warrant of Christianity is to be thought impossible. Trust and try. Attempt what God requires, and "account him faithful who has promised." If the work linger and seem every day more and more impossible, are we not then at the very point for Christian faith; for "hope against hope," in Him "who calleth those things that be not as though they were." Who shall dare to say that the Christian Patriarchs of the South, and the Christian

Philanthropists of the North, will not unite in seeking the aid of Heaven, and in Heaven's strength prevail, — fixing their eye, amidst the darkness and the storm, upon the only and sufficient encouragement ; — THE THINGS WHICH ARE IMPOSSIBLE WITH MEN ARE POSSIBLE WITH GOD.

WAREHAM, MASS., DEC. 1855.

CONTENTS.

CHAPTER I.

ADMISSIONS, DENIALS, DISTINCTIONS.

CHAPTER II.

THE PROBLEM OF AFRICA IN AMERICA.

CHAPTER III.

CLIMATE AND PRODUCTIONS OF THE SOUTH. — ORIGINAL AND ACTUAL CONDITION OF THE ENSLAVED RACE.

CHAPTER IV.

THE QUESTION TURNED TO WELL-BEING.

CHAPTER V.

AMERICAN EXPERIMENTS WITH BARBARISM.

CHAPTER VI.

EUROPEAN EXPERIMENTS WITH SERFDOM.

CHAPTER VII.

THE RESPONSIBILITY.

CHAPTER VIII.

IRRESPONSIBILITY OF THE UNITED STATES.

CHAPTER IX.

UNION BY SEPARATION.

CHAPTER X.

THE LAW OF EQUAL FORCES.

CHAPTER XI.

ADVANTAGES OF STATE SUPREMACY.

CHAPTER XII.

THE COMMON TERRITORIES AND FREE SOIL.

SLAVERY AND THE REMEDY.

CHAPTER I.

ADMISSIONS, DENIALS, DISTINCTIONS.

I BEGIN with the admission that slavery is an evil requiring a remedy; an evil both to the master and the slave. Without denying the larger share to the slave, the master's chains are scarcely less galling, and his sighs for relief are perhaps the more earnest of the two. "Our oppressed brethren at the South" are white as well as black. The slaves need to be released from the actual evils of their bondage to their masters, and the masters need to be released from the actual evils of their bondage to their slaves. No doubt slavery is an evil, imperiously demanding a remedy at once the best and the earliest possible — this year if you can; this day, this instant, if you can. If the slaves can be transformed into an industrious and thriving peasantry, and the masters into industrious and thriving proprietors, the sooner the better. Nothing can be more desirable than a code truly remedial; nothing can be more the absolute duty of a Christian state than to devise, enact, and execute such a code as speedily as possible.

Admitting, then, most distinctly, slavery as an evil requiring the earliest possible remedy, I deny it as a crime; as "a sin *per se*" at this present instant, *before* the earliest possible remedy. Slavery is ar. evil; and, of necessity, it is a sin to make a slave, or to make one's self a slave; but it does not follow that it is a sin to hold a slave. You are not responsible for an evil any further than you can prevent or cure it. You are not guilty for being a slave when you cannot help it by any right method ; neither are you guilty for being a slaveholder when you cannot help that by any right method. The entering voluntarily into slavery is a crime ; the bringing men into slavery is a crime. So is entering voluntarily into poverty, or bringing others into poverty, a crime ; but it is not, therefore, a crime to be poor, or to have poor neighbors. So it is with sickness and broken bones. It is a crime to make yourself or another man sick, to break your own or another man's bones ; but not to be sick, or have broken bones, or to be surrounded by the diseased and maimed until by all right methods you can make them whole and sound. It is not more a crime to be a slave until you can become rightly and advantageously free, or to hold other men in slavery until you can rightly and advantageously set them free from whatever galling bonds.

Expanding this common sense only on one side ; slave-holding, until slave-freeing can be accomplished rightly and advantageously, is not, cannot be a crime ; is not, cannot be a sin. It is wrong to enslave ; but slaves being found upon our hands, we are responsible, not for the enslaving, which occurred without our knowledge, and before our existence, but for remedying the evil as soon as we can.

To apply this to the opprobrious comparison of holding stolen goods : To steal is a crime ; to hold stolen goods *from* the owners *for* yourself is a crime. The partaker is as bad as the thief. But it is not a crime, but a virtue, to hold stolen goods in careful trust, in safe keeping, *for* the owner, to avail the utmost for his benefit. * * * A stolen looking glass ! a stolen watch ! What ! as soon as you know it, as quick as thought and muscle can act, are you to dash them on the pavement from the third loft, and glory in the speed with which you clear yourself of the guilt of holding stolen goods ? Far better hold them a day, a week, a year, ten years, if need be, in order to restore them most advantageously to the rightful owner. * * *

A stolen man ! found on your hands ! in your house ! What shall you do ? The goods are delicate, and may be injured or destroyed by over haste. Beware lest you kill or maim him in your hurry. File gently ; do not hew, lest in loosing his chains you mutilate or destroy. Do not toss him headlong from the uppermost window at the hazard of every bone in his body. Take time rather to lead him deliberately down stairs, through safe passages, that at least he may have a fair escape with life and limb as he goes from your hands, or you may incur a graver guilt than that of holding a stolen man.

Of course I deny the duty of immediate emancipation on the part of those to whom the question belongs; i. e., without such provisions and arrangements as require time — as must fit themselves gradually to the people concerned. "Institutions are not made, but grow." If I could persuade the legislatures of the slaveholding States to abolish slavery January 1, 1856, I would not do it. If I were autocrat, I would not decree it. I believe there is a more excellent way than immediate and unconditional emancipation. *Sat cito, si sat bene.* Soon enough, if well enough : too soon, if not well done.

In truth, immediate emancipation is impossible : however claimed in theory, it cannot be practically adopted. Every proposal and attempt carries in itself the principle of a necessary and righteous delay. Be it longer or shorter, there is an interval in which the master may and must remain a master — in which the slave may and must remain a slave. There is no ultra-abolitionist so utterly lost to all common sense as to deny that the individual master may delay, in order to such legal arrangements as shall secure and make advantageous the boon he confers; or that the State may take time to give form and scope to the enactments by which it undertakes to emancipate. There is an interval — be it longer or shorter, whether till to-morrow noon, January 1, or some more distant period — needful for a good and permanent result, as Christian discretion may decide. The crime is, the disobeying the rules for the interval, and deferring or neglecting the good and permanent result.

I do not forget the popular phrases assumed as establishing criminality, such as " the holding human beings as property;" " retaining the earnings of the slave;" but to me they seem to make the arguments in which they stand the merest fallacies — arguments from misnomers, as if they were true names; from words used in a peculiar, as if they had been used in the ordinary sense. " To insure life" is the most guilty presumption if the term be employed in its ordinary and not in its technical sense. " To sell the time" of a minor is arrogance and oppression if you take the words in any but the peculiar meaning which custom has settled, and then it may be as kind to him and his friends as it is just in you. "To hold human beings as property" is a crime when the terms are understood in the ordinary sense instead of that which custom has settled; and then it may be as right as it is unavoidable. The charge is a mere *criminatio verborum* without regard to the essential qualities of the act condemned, which, in the circumstances and for the time, may be a duty. Undoubtedly it is a sin to "hold men as property" without regard to the nature and relations of the goods, and then the sin lies in the criminal disregard. So it is folly to hold glass as property without due regard to the nature and relations of glass; but the folly lies in the disregard to its brittleness, and to the hard substances which expose it to be broken. It is both folly and crime to hold human beings "as property" without regard to physical, intellectual, social, and moral qualities and relations; but the folly and wickedness lie in that criminal disregard. So far is the idea of property, in its limited and peculiar sense, from being the essential quality of the sin, that the sin would be substantially the same if those attributes of men were not regarded among your free neighbors up to your power. If the African population were free you would hold your relation to them sinfully if you did not regard them in all their qualities and relations as men.

The condemnation for "withholding the earnings of the slave" is equally fallacious. "The slave does all the work, the master takes all the pay!" Does he indeed? Whence, then, another plea? viz., that free labor is more profitable than slave labor, because, forsooth, the slave gets a greater share of the pay than the freeman — more pay for less labor: his own maintenance, with that of his children and parents, and security for the future to boot! In truth, if the needs of the slave are duly cared for, the master does not "withhold the earnings of the slave." The capitalist, employing labor on such terms as custom authorizes, and the laws of capital require, — the only terms on which capital can for any length of time pay labor, — is, in respect to withholding earnings, precisely on the same footing as the slaveholder, with the exception that the merciful slaveholder has the worst of the bargain.

No doubt the capitalist, southern or northern, may withhold from labor its rightful earnings; and in either case let the judgment be according to the fault. But when the slave is provided for according to his wants and his master's means, then his earnings are not withheld, but bestowed just as truly as are paid the wages of the northern laborer.

Do we then make light of slavery, or become the advocates and upholders of every evil in connection with it? Alas, if we do! Let not the reader condemn us for these necessary distinctions until he has heard us through.

CHAPTER II.

THE PROBLEM OF AFRICA IN AMERICA.

THE evil of slavery admitted, the next preliminary in order to a remedial code must be *the settled fact of an Africo-American population.* The African race is established, and must be provided for chiefly on our soil. The evil is to be *remedied;* it cannot be removed. The problem of Africa in America is the problem to be solved.

The difficulties which beset the actual case are such that the theory of removal is undoubtedly the simplest and easiest. Yet, if only a theory utterly impracticable, it leaves the question of a remedial code on the spot to our earnest and determined, if indeed still our reluctant consideration.

That the African race cannot be removed, seems to me so plain as to supersede argument; as to need only to be asserted; all assumptions and projects to the contrary notwithstanding. Be it for good or evil, for weal or woe, the African race has become too numerous to be removed — cannot be removed *from* America *to* Africa so rapidly as to equal the natural increase, much less to exceed it. Nothing but some criminal check put in the way — some principle of decay and decrease introduced, added to compulsory and unmerciful transportation, can remove the one half of the natural increase. The evil must be remedied, not removed. The sooner this point is settled the better.

This assertion, needing no argument, might find argument in the facts which meet the writer as he repeats from an article published in 1820. " The Colonization Society is a noble institution, and in behalf of Africa we have no doubt will effect much ; but it will and must leave us an increasing black population. It is immensely important that we duly consider the subject, and enter without delay upon the best measures for reforming and improving a population which we must retain." More than one third of a century has passed, and how stands the assumption that needs no argument? The population which we began to remove has since then doubled its numbers — increasing very nearly in the same proportion as the white race, with all their advantages of a multitudinous immigration added to the natural increase.

Let the most favorable view be taken. Let it be supposed that the prosperity of Liberia shall become such as to make it the great point of attraction for the colored race ; that open space shall be found for the multitudes eager to emigrate, and that, whether by public aids or private means, emigration becomes as easy as a large European and American commerce has made that from the British Isles, what then can you expect? " The British Islands in the year 1792 contained a population of fifteen and a half millions. At the present moment the population is probably not less than thirty millions." *

The largest emigration which the world ever saw, finding room in every quarter of the globe, and borne on the wings of a universal commerce over every sea, has but doubled the population from which it has flowed. If America could send to Africa with equal facilities, and in the same proportion, she would but increase the number of her Africo-Americans, and at the end of sixty years would find the race doubled on her hands. It is time to awake from the dream of *removing*, to the earnest and determined work of *remedying* the evil.

All this is said in utmost friendship for the Colonization Society. Though it cannot remove or lessen the African population of this country, there are purposes which it is fitted to accomplish, and in its proper sphere it is worthy of all praise and coöperation. It may improve Africo-Americans by the responsibilities and privileges of Liberia on the one hand, and on the other by showing that the welfare of the African, like the European race, must be found not in the wealth or station of a favored few, but in the protected industry of the many. It may establish a civilized and Christian commonwealth on the coast of Africa, which shall aid in the abolition of the slave trade, and in extending civilization and Christianity

* See Blackwood's Magazine, March, 1845, and New York Observer, March 10.

over that wide continent. If it succeed in these high purposes, it is impossible to estimate its worth ; and even though it were utterly to fail, the attempt will not have been in vain.

It belongs to this chapter to demand *room* for the African race — room for their necessary increase and for their prosperous spread ; for an African as well as an American emigration ; a Southern West, suited to the Southern East, as well as a Northern West, suited to the Northern East. In a word, the territorial West cannot be disregarded in providing for the welfare of the African race. Their welfare is not to be secured by limiting them to their present boundaries, but by giving them the same room for expansion and improvement as the white race.

How this can be done in regard to the present slaves, or even the present free blacks, is a question not now requiring to be answered. We only demand at present, as a necessary condition of their wellbeing, room for expansion in connection with the white population of the South — a *belt of both races* from the Atlantic to the Pacific, now that both are to be considered as equally settled in the land.

The great southern statesman was right, not only in view of the welfare of the masters, but of the slaves, in claiming that the African race shall not be shut up within its present limits — that the South shall have an emigrating West for all its people as well as the North. All that can be required on the other hand is, that the emigration from the South shall carry with it no element of misery which a wise benevolence can cast off.

CHAPTER III.

CLIMATE AND PRODUCTIONS; ORIGINAL AND ACTUAL CONDITION

THE African race being considered as established, and to be provided for, chiefly on our soil, it must next be claimed that in our care for them we regard the climate and productions of the South, and the original and actual condition of the race.

As to climate and productions, this postulate is, of course, less and less needful, as we approach the line where the differences vanish. Applying ourselves to the comparison at distant points — to South Carolina and Massachusetts, for instance — it may be asserted, as impossible to establish northern equality at the South, under provisions and laws of nature which produce inequality; which would have produced it if social equality had existed at first, and which would reproduce and maintain it over any enactments to the contrary. Mr. Webster stated the case at Rochester in 1843, bringing the West Indies into comparison with New York. The nature of the crops, the production in one climate of what is wanted in all climates, and therefore requiring to be exchanged for the necessaries of life, destine them to commercial purposes, and not to immediate use. There must be cultivation and disposal on a large scale, with capital and proprietorship on the one hand, and employment and dependence, in a word, with service, on the other. If the South had been settled like the North, chiefly by one race; and had it begun its agriculture on the same scale of small proprietorship, the nature of the case would at length have brought to pass, in degree, the distinction which now prevails — capital and proprietorship on the one hand, and dependent service on the other; of masters and servants. This distinction will not vanish by any change in the institution of slavery, and any method of relief must regard it as unchangeable. Even if the African race could become sole possessors of the soil, by an equal subdivision, and with the energy and skill of the European race, the consequence would not be northern equality, but southern inequality. The smaller number would become proprietors, and the larger number dependent laborers, and the distinction would obtain among them of masters to be honored, and servants to honor, as in degree in all lands, and the special necessity in the culture and disposal of southern productions. Even the North does not, cannot carry its equalizing principle through society, but makes and shows like distinctions in proportion as it becomes in like circumstances; i. e., wherever capital and proprietorship have scope, as in the great commercial and manufacturing arrangements.

This social inequality, which cannot be prevented, it is still more difficult to set aside. If there were not the actual necessity, there is the actual fact, which it is impossible to annul, not only without violating all the rights of property, but to annul at all. So imperious is the actual fact, that even in northern countries it perpetuates itself, and admits only corrections and directions of what cannot be set aside. The abolition of slavery, and an agrarian law, could not annul what nature and Providence, what climate and time, have settled at the South.

But there is also to be regarded *the original and actual condition of the enslaved race.* The North is settled chiefly by the Anglo-Saxon race; whether superior by nature, or not, it is needless to ask. At the time of their emigration, they *were*, at this present, they *are*, farther advanced in civilization, more enterprising and persevering, with more science and art, with more skill and capital, and with the advantage in the main of a homogeneous population. The mere abolition of slavery, with the franchises of the North, and an agrarian law besides, would not give to the Africans of the South, at the instant, what they had not when they came, and have not now; what their fathers had not, and did not leave, as seed sown for their inheritance, viz., the enterprise, and perseverance, and skill, and capital of the white race. No law of equal privilege could remove the actual difference, any more than it could have removed the actual difference between the inhabitants of Great Britain and of the coast of Guinea a hundred and fifty years ago. In a word, if slavery has hindered the well-being of the slaves and of the whole South, it is not slavery merely. In degree at least, it is a lower civilization; a greater barbarism and poverty at the starting-point of emigration. The South less blessed than the North, because slavery has cursed them! and ready to be as blessed the moment slavery is abolished! Strange delusion! which forgets that almost half the population of the South were African barbarians, without enterprise, and perseverance, and skill, and capital, and therefore a dead weight, almost, upon the land which they came to inhabit. Many of the disadvantages of the South would have existed, if her African population had been free from the first; and would remain and grow, if an ill-advised and ill-regulated freedom were now to be bestowed.

Let it be supposed for a moment that the immigration of the southern negroes had been free; that the colonists from Africa, like the colonists from Europe, had come of their own accord, yet with the difference in fact existing between the Anglo-Saxon inhabitants of Great Britain and the inhabitants of the coast of Guinea. Can it be supposed that mere freedom would have put them and their posterity on an equality with the white race, and have given to the whole unhomogeneous South equal advantages with the homogeneous North? Must not the great mass of the African race have been " held to labor " by the race which was most advanced at the starting-point, and have found in that doom their best advantage; and the surest misery if they neglected or refused the boon? Nay, unless early and wise precautions had been employed, must there not have been a disadvantage to the State from the discordance of its original settlers? Would the African race have been at this moment an equal pillar of the public weal with the one half of the homogeneous people of the North? Surely it is not slavery alone which requires to be remedied, but evils which came with the race, and will remain after any mere decree of abolition, and which require a remedial code suited to the actual case.

The disadvantage supposed, even with a free African emigration, must of course have been enhanced by the special differences of the two races; such that they could not readily mingle and become homogeneous. No matter which race be of superior mould; it is enough that they are unlike — that the African is not equally agreeable to the European as his own blood, for other reasons besides color, in which they do not differ greatly from the straight-haired and fine-featured people of the East. The physical characteristics of the negro must have aided in dooming him to servile employments, in fixing him in the lower stratum of society, and at the same time in putting the whole southern community under the disadvantage of an unhomogeneous people, requiring peculiar remedies.

Nay, more; so certain is the operation of natural causes, that we may safely say, if the North had been under the same disadvantage of settlement, and had thence inherited even a free African population in the proportion of one third, neither that one third, nor the uncongenial mass, would show the present North as it now stands, in contrast with the present South. The contrast between Ohio and Kentucky, between New England and the Carolinas, had not been then as now. Millions of free blacks, free from their very emigration from the barbarism of Africa, with twofold as many millions of free Anglo-Saxons; — who can tell what might have been the disadvantage to either or to both? whether more or less than slavery itself has brought. Who can question that the North could not have been the North it is, if a good Providence had not given us a homogeneous and a civilized people, with small exception, from the first? And can any one think that slavery abolished, and the present slaves remaining free on southern soil, would put the South on the footing of the North? Nay, who dares to say that a free emigration of the African race into all our Anglo-Saxon franchises and privileges would not hinder or blast *our* prosperity even now? "The black code of Ohio" indicates a sense of exposure — is her acknowledgment that a "white code" does not provide for the wants of an unhomogeneous mass — is the acknowledgment of the North that a remedial code for the South must regard the original and actual condition of its servile race. There may be, and now that the difficulty exists, there must be, sought a method of relief; but there is an actual hinderance at the South in the incongeniality of its people. Carthage, under the disadvantage of bloods that would not mingle, could not cope with Rome, nor establish her own durable prosperity.* If we are allowed to hope for the future well-being of the South, notwithstanding the same disadvantage, it is because History and Christianity unite to give us a wisdom which Carthage had not — the wisdom to bless, in our midst, and with ourselves, a people whom we cannot remove.

* Arnold's Rome, Vol. II. Chap. XXXIX.

CHAPTER IV.

THE QUESTION TURNED TO WELL-BEING.

PRO-SLAVERY! ANTI-SLAVERY! And are these the only words which can meet the case of the servile population of the South, or of the mixed whole of masters and servants, bond and free? Are these the only words which can give direction to our discussions, and must we take part for the one or the other?

On the one hand, does the word *pro-slavery* fill the desire of the Christian patriarch, in behalf of his family around him? Does it satisfy a patriarchal State? Is the institution in its actual form, *slavery as it is*, so truly and completely patriarchal, as to be worthy to be retained and cherished, with whatever woe as well as weal, to both masters and servants, now and forever? On the other hand, does *anti-slavery* embrace all that the Christian philanthropist, all that the philanthropic State should seek, in order to carry out honestly and faithfully the command, " Thou shalt love thy neighbor as thyself"? Is anti-slavery, in its actual idea and programme, the desideratum for the enslaved race — for either race — for both races in their necessary dwelling together, so clearly, that it deserves to be the only and the headlong aim? Nay, do the Christian philanthropists, do the philanthropic States of the North, see anti-slavery and immediate abolition in so clear a light, with so sincere an eye, that they are ready to welcome to their own bosom a free negro population, in the proportion of one third or one half of the whole, without question as to the boon or the burden? as to the help or the hinderance of their future prosperity? as to the advantage even of that third, or moiety, itself?

Anti-slavery! pro-slavery! Is it absolutely settled that the parties who reproach each other with these names can have no other relation but as opposites and enemies? Is there not something to seek after, ay, and to find, which neither word signifies? *a question of well-being* superseding both, above and beyond both; in seeking which the Christian patriarch and the Christian philanthropist may earnestly and cordially unite?

The question, then, of *well-being*, and not of abolishing or retaining slavery, is claimed as the question which the Christian patriarch and philanthropist, which patriarchal and philanthropic States, have before them — a question just as open, as with regard to any other degraded and afflicted people on the face of the earth; each requiring an answer in view of their whole history and condition; suited at once to the great principles of justice and kindness, and to its own specific degradation and affliction. The question, What can be done for the well-being of the servile population of the South? is just as free for inquiry and discussion as concerning any other unfortunate portion of mankind — the Hindoos, the Chinese, or the present inhabitants of the coast of Guinea; each requiring an answer differing from the others, and all from the true answer for the Africans of the South.

Unhappily, this question of well-being is kept out of sight amidst the earnest discussions of the times. On the one hand, personal freedom is assumed as an absolute good, and in this "*petitio principii*" the great question of practical well-being is altogether overlooked, and with it the imperative duty, the glorious opportunity, of blessing the peculiar people on our hands, by philanthropic regulation and care; and on the other, slavery as it is, is claimed as the absolute necessity of the slaveholding States, instead of patriarchal amelioration, up to the point of that well-regulated freedom in which philanthropist and patriarch should meet. The Christian patriarch and the Christian philanthropist need not be at variance, if they will but unite in the simple attempt to promote the well-being of the slaves, in and with, as its only possible condition, the well-being of the whole people.

No doubt, in some sense, it were easier to cut all bonds and leave the slaves, set free, to shift for themselves as then best they might. But is this the method for a Christian State? for the Christian philanthropist and patriarch? Can the evils of slavery be rectified by the mere act of release? the mere loosing of bonds? without preserving whatever good may at present exist, and providing that the future may be safe and prosperous, according to our power?

Admit the evil to be such that no man can rightly reduce another man to slavery, any more than to poverty, sickness, or broken bones; admit that slavery as it is, has woes more than belong to a merely servile condition, and demanding the speediest possible remedy; it does not follow thence, that the whole condition of the enslaved requires to be changed, without discrimination of the evil and the good. You must remove the evil, but you must not remove the good; you must remove the injurious and destructive, but you must not remove the beneficial and conservative.

This duty of holding fast the good and casting off the evil only, is made imperative by manifest disabilities in the people whose well-being we seek; with the inheritance of less enterprise, and energy, and perseverance, and skill, and capital, than the Saxon race; nay, with less capacity of available labor than the myriad crowds from European lands, and incapable of competing with Irish and German toil. Have we nothing to do but to cut their bonds and leave them to themselves? Can we turn them off to be underbidden and overridden and oppressed, to be driven out before skill, and capital, and labor, miserable and destitute, to find their only relief in wasting from the earth, like the aboriginal freeman, the red man, before them? Can we release, not merely the slave from his master, but the master from his slave? Can a Christian State, philanthropic and patriarchal in very truth, release the master from his slave, without securing to the slave his labor and his pay; or the slave from his master, without securing labor *for* pay? A Christian State, philanthropic and patriarchal, is bound to abolish just so much of slavery as it is, as is injurious, and no more; to retain just so much as is beneficial, and no less; seeking in very deed the well-being of the enslaved race, and that common good in which alone their welfare can be found.

The Christian patriarch then, the patriarchal State, instead of cleaving to slavery as it is, will inquire if there are not points in which woe can be made less, and weal advanced; points of well-being to be regarded, which secured would change the meaning of the odious word, and exalt the slaveholder into a Christian patriarch. The Christian philanthropist also, the philanthropic State, instead of abolishing the institution, is bound to inquire whether emancipation at the instant, without conditions, will prove the remedy it seems; whether it might not abolish good as well as evil, and bring evil as well as good; might not miss points of well-being to the utter failure of the philanthropic intent; whether, slavery abolished and the slaves made free, those freemen might not find a doom which would crave the boon of a truly patriarchal slavery? The question is on things, not words; on substantial blessings, not empty names. Change the condition of the slaves into well-being; make slavery truly patriarchal, and the name will suit its meaning to the change. Emancipate the slaves into the freedom of the North, into competition with Anglo-Saxon enterprise, and energy, and skill, and capital, backed by European labor without count, and African freedom may come to mean the extremity of want and woe. The slaves deserve a better boon than such a freedom. Their rights forbid such a wrong. Their claims upon the soil require to be secured in the union of philanthropic and patriarchal care.

I cannot see that this claim of a right care and direction to be preserved, while all wrong care and direction are set aside, is at all forbidden by the fact that the negro race were brought into bondage by unquestioned wrong doing on the part of our predecessors, or even had it been by ourselves. If a piratical corsair, in mid-ocean, were to be visited by a Christian repentance, it could not demit all the authority with which it found itself invested, but would retain what was needful for the safety and welfare of its captives and the common good of all — the power to navigate and govern the ship, and bring her and her inmates to the haven. Christian repentance would forbid the giving up the ship to incompetent navigators, or the mixed society on board to anarchy and misrule. A repentant pirate would retain charge, and maintain authority; would give up the injurious and destructive; would preserve the beneficial and conservative.

But this demand of well-being is not to be understood as requiring security from all evils. That were a claim beyond not the doom only, but the needs of man; beyond the merciful intention to make this world a school of discipline. That were to contravene the decree, and the consolation, and the direction, and the benediction; "In the sweat of thy brow thou shalt eat bread; — The poor ye have always with you; — In this world ye shall have tribulation; but be of good cheer, I have overcome the world; — Faint not when thou art rebuked; — Bear ye one another's burdens; — Inasmuch as ye have done it unto one of the least of these my brethren, ye have done it unto me." No law of man, no preventive arrangement, no binding or loosing can set aside what God designs of want and suffering, and mutual aid and relief. Hunger, and thirst, and nakedness, and sickness, and calamity, and the care of providing for them, will remain, changing and interchanging in the most Christian communities, under the best productive and preventive regulations, philanthropic, patriarchal, to the utmost point; and this too, how far soever removed from that " over population," so wont to be assumed as the exponent of European woes. The law of human well-being is not, that mutual suffering and sympathy shall cease: no, neither with the high nor the low; neither with the rich nor the poor; neither with the master nor the slave. The rich are not exalted above — in many respects are exalted *into* wants and woes; the poor, whether they be few or many; the " masses " of the poor, are not depressed below the common ground of trial and of sympathy; giving as well as receiving relief. Such is human lot for human good; for the trial and strengthening of the suffering and relieving alike; for the forming of character, the true boon of this life, and the true preparation for the life to come. Neither the giver nor the receiver of the cup of cold water shall lose his reward.

Neither does our claim of well-being require release from all bonds. The principle, It is not good for man to be alone, belongs to all right, and to all rectified human obligations. The high cannot say to the low, the low cannot say to the high, the slave cannot say to his master, the master cannot say to the slave, I have no need of thee. The State has no wisdom, skill, nor power, that it can make its members free of each other. No decree, no law, can make man free of man, save by binding man to man, in mutual obligations. *Bonds make free.* Freedom from all bonds is the worst slavery. No community can make its members free, break whatever fetters, abolish whatever slavery it will, without retaining the bonds which unite men to each other; can emancipate the parts, without regarding the rules by which the whole can have a healthful subsistence. No community can make its members free to bread without the sweat of the brow; to wages, to " a living," without work; nor its casual or providential heads, its hereditary or its moneyed aristocracy, its lords, its masters, its employers of every grade, to be served without rendering a reward; to retain their capital without making it fulfil its proper function of providing labor and a living to their fellow-men; to luxurious enjoyment of the fruits of the earth without equalizing those fruits according to the relation in which they stand to their kind. The presumptuous franchise will destroy itself.

These great principles cannot be set aside in attempting a Remedial Code for the South. There are bonds to be retained on the master as well as on the slave, on the slave as well as on the master. The question is, What is for the well-being of the people? whether by bonds retained or by bonds loosed. Bonds make free, be they but righteous bonds. Freedom enslaves, if it be an unrighteous freedom. The poet's lesson, Be bold, be bold, reiterated and yet corrected, Be not too bold, may be applied to the indiscriminate and absolute claim for freedom. Be free; be free; be free; cannot be properly claimed of any people, save with that regard to its condition which shall give meaning and importance to the caution, *Be not too free!*

CHAPTER V.

AMERICAN EXPERIMENTS WITH BARBARISM.

In aid of our demand that well-being shall be the question, certain comparisons force themselves upon our consideration.

And first, *of the Africo-American with the aboriginal African.* Unquestionably Slavery, with its bonds upon the master and the slave, has afforded some facilities for promoting the well-being of such a people, for forestalling evils, for securing advantages which neither their native freedom nor an unconditional emancipation can give. Without withdrawing one iota from the just condemnation of the slave trade, the enslaving which began our woes, or of slavery as it is, it may be boldly claimed, That the facilities afforded by slavery have, notwithstanding its great and crying evils, actually improved and exalted the race. If still suffering from the barbarism from which they sprang, and therefore requiring methods different from the Anglo-Saxon race, most certainly they are not the barbarians they were; are not the barbarians which their African contemporaries are. African barbarism remains what it was two hundred years ago. African barbarism, translated and enslaved, has changed into comparative civilization, by the advantages and notwithstanding the disadvantages of slavery. The African of America is not so degraded as in our forgetfulness we allege; but has made large advance beyond the African barbarian from whom he sprang; beyond his cotemporary of the Coast of Guinea. The free African "kept down," "prevented from rising," by the influence of slavery, as is asserted; nay, the well-bred slave himself, and even the mass of Africans, bond and free, have actually risen far above their original degradation; have actually become more capable of labor, more industrious, more vigorous, more persevering, more skilful, wiser, than their cousins of Congo and Benin. Your educated preachers, your learned slaves, your eloquent advocates of emancipation, and, as truly, your diligent and faithful slaves in the field, and the house, and the shop, and the counting-house also, and your multitudes of thriving, discreet, capable Free Blacks, many no doubt in the lower, but not a few in respectable stations of life, give proof of the assertion over all the land. Africa in America is superior to aboriginal Africa. "The colored man is not a savage," says Dr. Channing in aid of his argument for freedom, "to whom toil is torture. Labor was his first lesson, and he has been repeating it all his life." The pleas for emancipation are grounded in part upon capabilities which slavery has produced.

This superiority claimed for the Africo-American, how does it show itself, now that he is carried back to the land of his fathers! America in Africa is superior to the proper Africa itself, and is giving proof of it before Europe and America, in a community capable of self-government, of regular industry, of the arts of civilization, of maintaining institutions of education and religion, of laying foundations and building thereon, of principles and progress. Says the Rev. J. Payne, Episcopal missionary at Cape Palmas, "The Amer-ico-African colonists, with all the disadvantages to which their social condition in the United States subjected them, are, to say the least, a century in advance of their heathen neighbors. Colonists fill already every civil office in Liberia, the higher ones most ably; why should they not, also, in time, fill all in the church?"* Says Rev. Mr. Miller, before a committee of the House of Lords, explaining the comparative advantage of Liberia over Sierra Leone with a much smaller expenditure, "Because Liberia is inhabited by a class of intelligent Christian negroes, while Sierra Leone is inhabited by recaptured Africans, who are little removed from the state of barbarism in which they were found by British cruisers."

But without authorities :— Let any one ask himself whether it had been possible to have formed a Liberia from aboriginal Africans? whether there could have been found among them the same power to form, and preserve, and make grow a prosperous State, as is found among the colonists from America, who, if "kept down" by slavery, have still most marvellously risen, giving proof that the principles by which they have been hindered, alone, are to be cast

* African Repository, May, 1849, p. 134.

aside, while those by which they have thus risen are to be most anxiously preserved. In a word, let the injurious and destructive be removed, but hold fast and cherish the improving and conservative; that instead of losing what they have gained, they may only add to their gains whatever they have lost.

Indeed, if in the inscrutable mystery of Providence there must needs be an Africo-American population — if the two races must needs meet in the new world; the civilized, enterprising, persevering, skilful and rich European, and the barbarous and destitute African as he was, and as the present aboriginal African is, must we not say: It was wisely ordered, that social and political supremacy was settled with the race actually most capable of its functions. If the African race is to belt the South, it is well that the supremacy remains, if only it be maintained in Christian wisdom and kindness, with patriarchal and philanthropic care; while yet, as in Liberia, there may be laid open for them chosen fields for the experiment of the highest social and political freedom.

But still another comparison forces itself upon us: I mean that of the Aboriginal American with the Africo-American. There are conservative and beneficial influences in slavery, under which the African barbarian has multiplied, and become in degree civilized and capable of the arts of life. *The North American Indian, left in his native freedom, has wasted and perished from the land of his fathers.*

Would we then have enslaved the Indians in order to preserve and exalt them? By no means. We justify neither Las Casas, who proposed negro slavery in order to keep the Indians free, (for he did not justify himself,) nor the colonists whose wrong-doing prompted the mistaken kindness of the father. Neither do we see clearly how a beneficial conservatism and restraint could have been undertaken in behalf of American savages. And yet from the double experiment of slavery and freedom, and their contrasted issues, we may learn to look, where we have the power and opportunity, for something better than unconditional emancipation, than the abolition of the tried and proved elements of African well-being. After having destroyed (almost) the one race of barbarians because they were too free, we will beware of removing the bonds by which we have actually preserved, extended, and in very deed improved and exalted the other.

I know how easily it may be said, "The Indians are doomed to disappear before civilized men:" how easily *Fate* may be assumed as the explanation of the melancholy fact. With like wisdom it was said once, *Nature abhors a vacuum*, until the discovery that Nature's abhorrence was limited to thirty-two feet; above which, *Nature liked a vacuum.* Nature, fate, or what not, *likes a vacuum* of savages in connection with the civilized, if they be red and straight-haired, but abhors it if they be black and woolly-headed! Strange freaks of Nature! and strange philosophy! How much better to say, Barbarians, if they can be "held to labor," trained and ruled to diligence, order, regularity, under the example of a civilized and Christian community, may be preserved and multiplied, and trained; may grow progressively in well-being; while freedom, idleness, and vice, will prove their ruin. Out of the fiction of the abhorrence of a vacuum, we get nothing but disappointment as we dig; out of the experimental induction of the pressure of the atmosphere, how are we enriched with science and art! From the fiction of a doom upon the Aboriginal American, comes nothing but wholesale destruction of savage tribes; from the conclusions of experience, what results may we gain of African well-being, belting our own land, and transplanted that it may overspread Africa itself. An ameliorated slavery — a well-regulated freedom, call it by whichever name you will, with scope to aspire after the highest franchises, is the true conclusion from American experiments with barbarism.

CHAPTER VI.

EUROPEAN EXPERIMENTS WITH SERFDOM.

I DO not forget the rebuke to which I expose myself; the popular ban of the Nineteenth century upon the claim of bonds to make free — of an ameliorated slavery instead of unconditional abolition; as if there were some magic in the number of the age. The Nineteenth century indeed! And what is there in that charmed number which can deliver it from the lessons of all preceding centuries — from learning its wisdom from all time? which forbids it to read the ripened history of ages, and to find therein the lessons of present wisdom; made plain as proverbs to the intuition of the age, though it were in such words as ours: Bonds make free: Be not too free. The Nineteenth century is not to be controlled in the testimony it bears, in the direction it gives. Instead of requiring unconditional emancipation, it may be found, when its voice is fully and rightly heard, to require bonds retained as well as loosed. The Christian philanthropist must trace modern evils to their sources; must receive modern wisdom in its fulness, from the contributions of all times. When the river has refused and cast off the streams from every spring-head and lake, it is but a cup full or a drop. Whatever heedless philanthropy there be, boasting itself of new wisdom, is itself "behind the times." They only who welcome the lessons of experience have the true wisdom of the age.

An ounce of prevention is worth a pound of cure. The abolition of serfdom, brought about by the influence of Christianity, wanted nevertheless important elements of Christian wisdom. "The misery of the masses," and the concurrent misery of property and capital; nay, the very chaos of society; the mutual suffering of all classes, and the dread of coming evils, making men's minds to fail for fear, do but confirm the assertion: Bonds make free. Too free a freedom was bestowed upon lords and serfs together; too many bonds were loosed for the well-being of either, for the well-being of the whole. *Serfs and lords would have been mutually more free if they had been mutually more bound.* Let not the paradox be hastily discarded.

Before loosing all bonds, whether of master or slave, the Nineteenth century should ask of the centuries which have gone before, whether, in solving its great problem, the preventive ounce may not prevail against the pound which modern Europe shows hindering or baffling cure. There can be no question that the serfdom of the middle ages did in degree provide food, and raiment, and shelter, and safety to the mass in exchange for labor, the degree varying according to the interests and character of the lord; that serfdom gave some blessings which *mere* freedom would take away; that it required and even secured some duties from the lords which an inconsiderate release might leave in neglect. If those mutual obligations which bind together the high and the low, be disregarded, the presumptuous franchise will destroy itself. The iniquity and the folly will be visited on successive generations. There will be "miserable masses," baffling relief, because too little "held to labor," and too little sustained by the laborer's hire; and miserable property, also, a miserable hereditary or moneyed aristocracy, because property and rank did not cherish labor, did not benefit and comfort the laborer. In a word, society will be less free for the want of mutual bonds. An ounce of prevention is worth a pound of cure. In giving freedom to the slave, be sure that you do not enslave him to the "misery of the masses" of the nineteenth century — to want and woe. In giving freedom to the master, be sure that you do not enslave *him* to possessions which curse the possessor. Be sure, in your zeal, that you do not take away from the slave the points of well-being which his very slavery secures; nor from the master the salutary obligations of his lot. Do not release the slave without providing for his future support *by* his labor; nor the master, without requiring him to yield that support *for* labor.

The great social law of mutual interdependence cannot change — cannot be broken with impunity by the master more than by the slave; by property and capital more than by labor. The law and the penalty are divinely declared in the imprecation of the Prince of Uz : * "If my land cry against me, or the furrows thereof com-

* Job xxxi. 38.

plain; if I have eaten the fruit thereof without money, or have caused the owners thereof to lose their life; let thistles grow instead of wheat, and cockle instead of barley;"—in the prophet's warning:* "Hear ye this, ye which oppress the poor, which crush the needy; the Lord God hath sworn by his holiness that, lo! the days shall come upon you, that he will take you away with hooks, and your posterity with fish-hooks;"—in the apostle's denunciation:† "Go to now, ye rich men, weep and howl, for your miseries that shall come upon you. Your riches are corrupted, and your garments are moth-eaten. Your gold and your silver is cankered, and the rust of them shall be a witness against you, and shall eat your flesh as it were fire. Behold the hire of the laborers who have reaped down your fields, which is of you kept back by fraud, crieth, and the cries of them which reaped are entered into the ears of the Lord God of Sabaoth." *The presumptuous franchise destroys itself.* Surely the abolition of serfdom wanted some elements of Christian wisdom when it made property too free of obligation to maintain labor, and labor too free of obligation to sustain property; and "miserable masses," and property encumbered with woes and fears, have been the consequence.

Whatever difficulty there may be in the illustrations required, there are some obvious points in the condition of Europe as connected with the abolition of serfdom, to which we shall do well if we take heed in attempting a remedy for American slavery. In avoiding the points in which Christian Europe has failed, we may find the true amelioration, the rightly-regulated freedom, the very method of well-being, the preventive ounce, against miseries which cannot be weighed. ‡

---

* Amos iv. 2.

† James v. 1.

‡ The refusal to entertain the question of well-being, and the insisting on the absolute and immediate abolition of slavery, is the more remarkable in view of the strange projects for relief which the disastrous issue of the European experiment has called forth; in view of the *new slavery* proposed in remedy of the "misery of the masses." Strange to see! At the very moment when we are so urgent for unconditional emancipation in America, the miseries of the free in Europe are looking for relief to new forms of servitude. The great problem of European revolutionists is, *How to provide for unenslaved masses by enslaving them again!* — what new chains to impose in order to secure the well-being of the people! * * * Strange to see!

Looking, then, to the European experiment, what learn we for our guidance?

And first, from France? from her condition before the revolution of 1789, producing that revolution, with its horror and dismay? the miseries of the low, and the still greater miseries of men of high estate? from the imperfect remedy under the consulate and empire? under the restored dynasty of 1815? under the revolution of 1830? under the volcano and burning lava of 1848, with all its issues and uncertainties? Whatever may be due to other causes, who can fail to trace the wants and woes of the high and the low, the rich and the poor, the lord and the serf, as they were sixty years ago, and in all their varied forms, up to the present hour, to *that too free a freedom* which for some centuries took place of the ancient serfdom, of the *mutual bonds*, which, with many evils, had secured some blessings unto all?

Whatever difficulties may belong to a subject so variously related, we may confidently refer the destitution and misery of the lower orders in France before the revolution, and of course the subsequent miseries of the higher, in part, *to the too great freedom of the lords* to live where they pleased, and how they pleased, without regarding in their place and expenditure the advantage of the laborers on the soil; expending in the luxury and dissipation of the capital the fruits of labor, instead of with the laborer, in just payment, and generous oversight and care; and to the uncertain and oppressive

In countries more favorably situated for emancipation than our own; where there was neither incongeniality of race, nor floods of immigrating labor; neither the difficulty found by the negro in connection with the Saxon from the first, nor the new flood of Saxon and Celt upon the fields of toil, personal freedom has ended in such " misery of the masses," in such horrible and general destitution as makes men ask for bonds in order to an available freedom; and in such misery of an hereditary and moneyed aristocracy also; in such difficulties, and overthrows, and anxieties, and dismay, as have made the whole world stand aghast. How significant the sanction to the demand! — Be not too free; Bonds make free, — found in the new and mistaken slavery, in place of the too free personal freedom which preceded. Names do not alter things. Words of freedom cannot make the modern devices other than a new slavery in remedy of the ills brought in by freedom too absolutely abolished — of the evils of too free a freedom. Under the plausible names of fraternity, equality, socialism, what is called for but regulation, restriction, direction, *bonds*, in regard to labor, time, place, capital, property, hitherto too free?

taxation, and restrained and discouraged industry of this neglected peasantry. No wonder that misery ripened upon the poor and the rich together, when the sweat of the brow could no longer earn bread, and the cries of " hire kept back by fraud " had "entered into the ears of the Lord God of Sabaoth." In 1789, the rural laborer of France was declared by Arthur Young to be seventy-six per cent. poorer than that of England; the French peasant not one fourth as well provided as the English peasant; " less at his ease, worse fed, worse lodged, worse clothed — reminding one of the miseries of Ireland." * How soon followed the reverses due to neglectful and unjust property and capital, until they were " fished with hooks," and posterity, and again posterity, " with fish-hooks," for the violation of the great social law of mutual interdependence among men !

The like connection is to be traced in the miseries of Ireland, comparable in 1789 with the miseries of France, and seventy-six per cent. below the miseries of England; for why, then, for why continuing and growing until now? For why? if not because property and capital have not performed their functions for labor, and because labor has not performed its duty to property and capital? or, fixing upon two obvious points; in part, because Ireland was not blessed with either advantage of the " poor laws " of Elizabeth, viz., provision for the absolutely needy and incapable, and the demand of labor from those able to work; and in part because *non-residence* has defrauded labor of both wages and care. Thus those whom property and capital have forsaken, and who have also been idle and negligent themselves, have perished by thousands, almost without hope of relief, and the abused property and capital are cankered in the hands of their possessors, and " eat their flesh as it were fire." An impoverished tenantry must make an impoverished aristocracy. The " evictions " of miserable thousands, and the horrors of enraged hunger; valueless estates, or estates to which assassination and murder are entailed, may be referred, in part, to too many bonds loosed — too few bonds retained.

That the principles of Irish misery may be the more manifest, it stands *in striking contrast with Irish well-being,* where for many generations property and capital have been faithful to their func-

---

* Wealth of Nations, Book III. Chap. II.

tions; where pay has provided and rewarded labor, and where labor, also, has been rendered for pay. Happily the experiment of James I. has been called up to give wisdom to the nineteenth century for the recovery of an afflicted and desolate people on the better principle of keeping on the soil, and restoring thereon, a ruined peasantry, instead of substituting another people in their place.

"It is now nearly two hundred and forty years," says Sir Robert Peel, "since a Sovereign of this country, desirous of making a settlement in Ireland, sought the assistance of the city of London. He invited their coöperation in restoring what were then called the ruinated cities of Londonderry and Coleraine. If there be any party in this country which has reason to look back with pride on Ireland, and its connection with Ireland, it is the city of London. It is the city of London which has done more than parliament or proprietors to promote the interests of that country; which has forgotten the consideration of temporary gain, which has forgone present interest, which has sought a compensation for these sacrifices, by promoting the permanent welfare of the district with which it was connected. I hope, after the lapse of two hundred and forty years, that the city of London may be enabled again to promote the welfare of that country. It will act now upon other views, more liberal — more comprehensive than before. It will not seek, as it heretofore did, to expel the natives from the soil. It will seek to elevate their character, to encourage their industry, to find for them permanent employment, to instil the principles of order, of respect for the laws, of submission to authority." "But for Ulster," says the London Times, commenting on Sir Robert Peel, "but for Ulster, we should scarcely have hope. The estates of the city of London are an oasis in that social and almost physical waste. The cost of the plantation probably did not exceed the contributions of London alone, to one year's expenses of the Revolutionary war. But the work still endures, flourishes and expands. * * * It bids fair to last out the world, so that to the end of time, a cultivated country and a prosperous people will be a living record of the plantation of Ulster under James I."

If the peasantry of England might be deservedly ranked far above that of France in 1789, or of Ireland at this moment, there, also, without question, those mutual bonds needful to make freedom avail to the personal and social well-being of all classes, fail in degree; while, nevertheless, the better condition of the lower orders in England, and of England on the whole, is due in part to mutual bonds retained. There may be a question, indeed, connected with the "poor laws" of Elizabeth, whether a too certain and easy claim upon the property and capital of the country may not in some degree have promoted the pauperism for which they intended only to provide; but there can be no question that those laws, along with a better encouraged industry,* were bonds on property and capital — on the aristocracy, on the masters in favor of the released serfs of earlier times; such as have made the peasantry of England for centuries, in better condition than that of either France or Ireland. This advantage is due partly to direct relief; partly to an indirect influence stimulating the people to provide for themselves, and partly, perhaps, to the tendency of this tax upon property to prevent non residence, to promote residence, and thus to add sympathy, and counsel, and care, and voluntary aid, and an advantageous expenditure, to the provision furnished directly by the laws.

If this asertion be just, how much more would its justice appear, if, with the bonds on property and rank, there had been enforced the bonds on labor, also, for which those same "laws of Elizabeth" provided. In the words of Blackstone, their object was, not only "First, to raise competent sums for the necessary relief of the poor, impotent, old, and blind, and such other, being poor and not able to work;" but also, "Secondly, to provide work for such as are able and cannot otherwise get employment," or in other words, "to relieve the impotent poor, and them only, and to find employment for such as are able to work." "But this latter part of the duty," adds Blackstone, "which according to the wise regulations of this salutary statute, should go hand in hand with the other, is now most shamefully neglected." If both parts had been duly observed, how truly would there have been mutual bonds on property and labor, that both might have been thereby more free: — a substitute for the advantages of serfdom, and the care of the monasteries, by which all the members of society would have been benefited; worthy the commendations of the great commentator on the English law: — "A plan was formed in the reign of Queen Elizabeth, more humane and beneficial than even the feeding and cloth-

* Alison's Europe, Chap. II.

ing of millions, by affording them the means, with proper industry, of feeding and clothing themselves:" * the whole on the great principle of these papers, of mutual bonds in order to mutual freedom ; thus stated by Blackstone in connection with these laws of Elizabeth: "There is not a more necessary, or more certain maxim in the frame and constitution of society, than that every individual must contribute his share, in order to the well-being of the community ; and surely they must be very deficient in sound policy who suffer one half of a parish to continue idle, dissolute, and unemployed, and at length are amazed to find that the industry of the other half is not able to maintain the whole."

The lesson is plain ;—What might have been done easily with the ounces, has become impossible since they have grown to pounds and to tons. Or, varying the figure ; what might have been done with the sapling, is impossible with the full grown and gigantic trunk. What Europe could have prevented by due bonds on property and labor, when both were in the manageable state of the middle ages —what she might have done by an ameliorated serfdom, must be utterly beyond her power when all the facilities of the ancient system have passed away, and the work to be done has increased a thousand fold. The full grown miseries of centuries will not be removed by forces which might have availed in their infancy. The ancient oak will not be handled as if it were a sapling.

And now, summing up the examples referred to in this chapter and the last :— the improvement of the African race, under certain advantages, amidst the disadvantages of slavery ; the deterioration and wasting away of the American aborigines, under certain disadvantages, amidst the advantages of freedom ; and the "misery of the masses," with the concurrent misery of property and capital in Europe, for the lack of mutual bonds, illustrate the assertion — Bonds make free ; and justify the all important claim, that well-being shall be the question with regard to the slaves and masters of the South, whether by bonds loosed or bonds retained. The proprietor, the capitalist, the lord, the master, may "do what he will with his own," may live where he will, and how he will, only with due regard to the laborers who depend upon him ; or his freed wealth shall be worse to him than wholesome poverty itself. The

* Commentaries, B. 1. Chap. IX.

ancient serf or the modern slave may be made free of whatever bonds, and yet only in due regard to property and capital, to proprietor and capitalist, the natural helpers of labor, or his freedom will be less desirable than an ameliorated slavery. The presumptuous franchise of labor without pay, or pay without labor, will destroy itself.

If this view be just — if bonds were needful to be retained, hundreds of years ago, when the liberty given was that of Europe, how much more now, when the emancipation proposed is into personal and political liberty, as it exists, full grown, on American soil.

Granted, that the freedom of the North, personal and political, inherited from our English ancestors two hundred years ago, and full grown since, on the soil of the New World, is fitted to its place and people, and that it can even assimilate a multitudinous European emigration, so perfectly, that from age to age we shall be a homogeneous Republic, with no portion of the assimilated mass incapable of co-acting with the whole : —

Does it follow thence, that even the nations of Europe in their place, and with their people — above all, does it follow that a race so different as the Negro, can be thus made free ? — that such a freedom could be established and maintained ? — that such a freedom would not become their worst bondage ? Does it follow that we can decree our freedom to them, as they have been, and are ? that we can emancipate them into what we enjoy ? that we can make for them in a day what God has made for us in centuries ? that it can be theirs, until, as with us, it unfold itself as the slow growth of ages ? that with us they can retain it, or if we were to vanish from the soil, could hold it for themselves ? Miserable delusion ! to think that you can call forth the full grown and solid oak, except by the process by which the acorn unfolds and strengthens itself, year after year, and age after age : — to take the last result of centuries of discipline, and expect to build it up in Europe by a three days' *emeute*, or among three millions of Africo-Americans, by some decree of enfranchisement, some day of universal emancipation. Better far if that boon can be found, an ameliorated slavery, which shall prove itself a well regulated freedom ; better, far, to deal with the ounces, than to hazard the pounds and the tons, which no strength can lift ; to handle the sapling, than to wait for the full grown and enormous trunk of the twenty-second century.

The writer does not presume that he has accomplished the grand desideratum. His utmost hope is, that he has made an imperfect attempt in the right line, and may render some small aid in recalling his misguided countrymen from the wrong lines designated by the terms "pro-slavery" and "anti-slavery," from mutual reproaches about opposite impracticables, to union in seeking a practical good. He invokes the wisdom of the country, philanthropic, patriarchal, to the utmost point, to perfect a method of well-being for the slaves, in and with the well-being of the European race — a method of well-being for our whole country, suffering and blessed together, in the suffering and blessing of each several member of the united body.

With this hope, how might the philanthropist and patriarch weep in bitter repentance over the long refused opportunity — the long delayed wisdom! What if this had been the attempt of the last twenty years, not to abolish slavery ; not to set the slave free of his master, or the master of his slave, but whether by binding or loosing, to promote the well-being of both and of the whole — the Nineteenth century drawing this wisdom from all previous time. What if the Christian philanthropists of the North, and the Christian patriarchs of the South had united in this good attempt ; instead of clamor and anti-clamor, and jar and discord, making sweet harmony through all the land. How then may we suppose the evils of slavery already removed. and the blessings with slavery retained ; freedom established which is freedom indeed, suited to the actual condition of both races, of which we have said, Bonds make free ; the thing without the name, against and above all counter names ; liberty, equality, fraternity, in all the real good which those abused words can suggest ; without the anarchy, and overthrow, and bloodshed, and anxieties, and dreads, in the train of a false and flattering philanthropy ; a pattern to the European world, in recovering from the miseries of too free a freedom, and giving to the Nineteenth century a glory which should not pass away. * * *

If we find a method for the well-being of slaves and slaveholders, it may suggest a method for the well-being of "miserable masses," so true to the law of mutual interdependence, so true to the unalterable relations of property and labor, as shall repair the damage of too free a freedom, and bless all orders of society together "Bonds that make free" may come to be encouraged by American example.

CHAPTER VII.

THE RESPONSIBILITY.

THE appeal is, necessarily, to a *sense of responsibility*. If this is not to be found, if it cannot be roused, then discussion, illustration, proposal, urgency, whether in regard to emancipation or well-being, are in vain. Of course the appeal for well-being is not to be put down, and that for emancipation set up, on the assumption that there is *no* sense of responsibility, or that no sense of responsibility can be roused; — that slaveholders, that the "South," are so absolutely selfish and unjust, so void of conscience, that discussion, illustration, proposal, urgency for the *well-being of the slaves,* is utterly useless. For ourselves, *we* believe not only that there is an actual and fearful responsibility, in regard to the three millions of slaves, and the twenty millions with whom they are connected, and to the geometric ratio of the future, but a sense of it at the South, and among slaveholders to be appealed to, and to be more and more aroused, until the desire of philanthropist and patriarch shall be fulfilled in the well-being of the people, whether bond or free. However this may be, whatever and wherever the sense of it, there is a responsibility of which we are now to speak.

And this responsibility is to God, for man. Let it be set forth as it is, with no diminution because it relates to Africans and slaves, and to those who stand to them in the relation of masters. The responsibility is to God, and to his perfect law : to the great law of truth, and justice, and kindness, which is to regulate the doing of man to man, with all the sanctions which belong to the breach and the observance, here and hereafter. The remedy of a great social evil, the provision for a great social good, is not to be accomplished save in reference to the highest sanctions of human conduct, save in reference to the supreme authority over man. " The wisdom of Numa " was not in vain, has not been in vain, in recovering and establishing states — has been every where acknowledged, pagan though it was, as better than atheistical philosophy, than philosophic indifference. Let it not be supposed that Christian nations can find an Atheistical wisdom; can obtain a durable prosperity, without a conscientious righteousness. We have no remedy to propose, no appeal to make, which shall supersede a regard to the Supreme Ruler, and the supreme law.

But there are limits to this responsibility. The astronomer is mad who burdens his conscience with the charge of winds, and clouds, and rains, and sunshine, and their influence upon the harvests by which man and beast must live. The philanthropist is mad who burdens his conscience with accomplishing his own estimate and plan for the well-being of his race; who undertakes to overrule the great Overruler himself. The responsibility — the sense of responsibility claimed and appealed to, in regard to the well-being of the African race in and with the well-being of the whole community — is to do what can be done; is for right and wise attempts, and for all that success which a good Providence may give. There is no responsibilty for impossibilities. There is no responsibility to remove all evils, and secure all benefits, to equalize all conditions; for that were a responsibility which exists not in regard to any nation on the face of the earth, and would destroy the school of discipline which God has appointed — would overrule the great Overruler. There are limits to human responsibility, and there is no responsibility beyond them. There is no responsibility to annul the laws of inequality in the varying conditions of men — to contravene the decree, " The poor ye shall always have with you," to be provided for by wages or by charity. Not emancipation from all bonds, not an Agrarian law, not a theoretic, not an absolute equality, are required of human responsibility. The Christian equalization is on the very principle of inequality; suited to the varying scene of human wealth and want, which human discipline requires; is made by justice and kindness freely moving amidst human inequalities, amidst suffering and relieving men; by means of which, " he that gathereth much hath nothing over, and he that gathereth little hath no lack ;" in which the full prepare a harvest for their own necessities by sowing to those who are in want. There is, there can be, no responsibility to institute to-day, out of African elements, a British or American condition — to make the two divisions of population of South Carolina into the homogeneous mass of Massachusetts. The responsibility is to do what can be done for the well-being of the people as they are, whether by bonds loosed or bonds retained, as truth, justice, kindness may require.

The responsibility, thus defined and distinguished, belongs, of course, first and chiefly, to the slaveholders, individually and socially. Each master is personally responsible to do all he can, under and with existing laws, both in the current care of those with whom he finds himself charged, and in making the best possible arrangements for their future welfare, whether during or after his own life. Whatever hindrance may be found in existing laws, he is bound to provide against to his utmost powers. Whatever the State may do or leave undone, there is a personal responsibility for the interval of its delay, according to whatever powers and facilities remain.

But especially society is responsible for a great social evil; the State, that mysterious personality, so difficult to define, but which the supreme Ruler holds to account; — not expressed by the monarch's presumption, " I am the State;" or by the republic's pride, " We govern ourselves;" — the State, which the King of kings knows where to find and how to reward: the boastful head and the boastful members having their mysterious share in the social responsibility, whether by political action or inaction, by interest or indifference, by approval or disapproval. The evil is social and political, and the remedy must be social and political also. The sovereign State must provide for the evils of the State; must open the way for the responsible action of all its members for the common good. What is every body's business is nobody's. It is not enough to say that every individual is responsible, while yet nobody is left distinctly and solemnly accountable. The State itself is the personality of which arrangements wise and salutary must be claimed, in that corporate and distinct existence by which it is a State, in whose unity all the members are mysteriously and inseparably joined.

The State, then, in its corporate capacity, — government growing out of the necessities and moral sensibilities of men; the child of the past, the nurse of the present, the parent of the future; which God has ordained, and which no royal presumption or democratic pride can wrest from His hands; — each sovereign State is responsible to do all that its existing constitution admits, and to adopt into its constitution whatever needful powers.

The State responsible, thus, for the use and extension of its powers, must act through official persons, its necessary organs, legislative, executive, judicial, for and with the whole body of which they are the organs. Official persons, the organs of the State, are themselves responsible, not as individuals merely, but as public organs, for all the opportunities and powers which belong to their offices severally, — not to their appointees principally, to their instructions or complaints, but to the Ruler of rulers, to do what he requires of them as the organs of a Christian State:

> " Among the rulers of the earth
> A greater Ruler takes his seat:
> The God of heaven, as Judge, surveys
> Those gods on high, and all their ways."

But there are limits to the responsibility of the State, as there are limits to its sovereign power. It is bound to do what it can and no more; what it has a right and ability to do and no more. Its organs, legislative, executive, judicial, are responsible only for what is right and possible to them as the organs of the State; to act with and not against the constitution of the State whose organs they are; to act, also, according and not contrary to the materials on which they have to act; with and not without just consideration of all the relations in which they stand to the past, the present, and the future; in view of all the helps and hindrances which belong to the nature of men, ay, and to the very kinds and classes with whom they have to deal, and to the nature of the State whose organs they are — at once the child of the past, the nurse of the present, and the parent of the future, — regardful of the stream of custom and prescription which cannot be instantly created or destroyed; which cannot be turned in its present fulness into new channels, without ruin and desolation in its course.

Fixing, thus, chiefly, the responsibility upon slaveholders and the slaveholding States, in their separate sovereignties, it must still be claimed that there is a responsibility beside, or else the writer has no claim to a hearing, — is mistaken in his deep sense of duty. No doubt, within proper limitations, there is a responsibility at the North as well as at the South, — in every northern State and in every northern man, — just as we are responsible for the relief of misery the wide world over, according to our relations and our powers, to do what in us lies for the benefit of our fellow-men : not to govern where God and nature have given no authority, but in every way to aid and comfort in agreement with the laws of God and nature. There is no evil on the face of the earth which may not be rightly discussed, and for which just relief may not be attempted by any man on the face of the earth There is no sovereign State so sovereign, no monarchy on a throne so high, no republic in its amassed supremacy so supreme, that it may not be confronted, ay, and roused, and reclaimed, and blessed by " that same poor man." The humblest American may speak to the proudest of the American States. Man *to* man may speak *for* man, under no other restrictions but to speak the words of truth, and justice, and kindness, as a Christian philanthropist, and no man or people has the right to gainsay. *Homo sum, humani nihil a me alienum puto.*

CHAPTER VIII.

IRRESPONSIBILITY OF THE UNITED STATES.

RESPONSIBILITY there is, no doubt, as upon every citizen, so upon the United States, to do what in us lies for the well-being of the whole South, but " not to govern, where God or nature has given no authority; " not to do, what in us does not lie, to regulate or abolish slavery in the States. These assertions are presumed to agree with the general sentiment of the country, and yet there are not wanting scruples and evasions, pretensions and attempts, which require that the irresponsibility of the United States should be carefully stated and illustrated. And this not only to check useless interference, but to quicken the sense of the actual responsibility. If the responsibility is *not* on the United States, it *is* tremendously upon each separate State. The plea against action in the General Government does not lighten the charge of three millions of men and their posterity, which Divine Providence has laid upon the responsible States — is *for* action " with no diminution because it relates to Africans and slaves," " not indeed to loose all bonds, but whether by bonds loosed or bonds retained, to seek their well-being in and with the well-being of the whole people."

Still deferring our conception of the detail, our view of a Remedial code; nothing can be more certain than the necessity of some specific and appropriate legislation for a peculiar race settled with us beyond removal, some great and comprehensive measure of Police. Such a legislation, at once merciful and just, regardful of property and labor, suited to man, providing for the well-being of both races, worthy of the Christian philanthropist and the Christian patriarch alike, how would it prove the glory of the South and the joy of the North; the oil of gladness and the dew of refreshing upon an indissoluble Union!

In the hope of contributing to this result we proceed to state and to illustrate the irresponsibility of the United States. We disclaim, then, utterly, all right in the United States to interfere with the separate States as to slavery. Whatever the duties of the States may be in their separate sovereignties, these are not the duties of the United States; not more than they are the duties of any other government on the face of the earth; not more than of Great Britain or France. Of course, the Congress of the United States has no duty of interference, more than the British Parliament or the French Legislative Assembly; and the citizens of the United States as citizens, have no duty of interference more than the citizens of Great Britain or France. We have not even the " right of petition" thereon : i. e. we have no right to move the United States to do what they have no right to do. The right to petition cannot extend beyond the right to act. To petition Congress in the matter, would be as inconsistent and absurd as to forward petitions to London or Paris. Be the evil ever so great, be the duty of the separate States ever so imperious, whether of abolition or amelioration, neither Washington, London, nor Paris, can be urged to interfere. Whatever the evil or the wrong of slavery, God has given the United States no authority in the matter. The great Overruler has so overruled as to limit our right and our power, as to prevent our responsibility.

There are two questions concerning the responsibility of the United States. The one as *under* the Constitution, the other as *for* the Constitution itself, and for whatever alterations. It is not enough to say, we are not responsible under the Constitution, unless we can also say, we are not responsible for the Constitution. All that regards the former question will be sufficiently considered under the latter.

We are not responsible then, for giving to the Slave-holding States the powers they have. We did not give what we might have kept. We are not continuing what we have the right and power to reclaim. There is an illusion in the popular phrase, "the compromises of the Constitution." Neither the North nor the South seem to understand that their relations to each other were not their independent choice; that they exist not at their pleasure, that they cannot be altered at their will. The Constitution is not a guilty compromise in regard to slavery, to be repented of and set aside by the North; is not to be held fast at the South, as a charter by mutual consent, but is to be retained by both, as a conformity to our actual condition; to the grounds and necessities of our political state. The national sovereignty not only finds no responsibility in those delegated powers by which it is constitutionally sovereign; but it finds none in those circumstances, those progressive events above human foresight or control, producing and illustrating its powers and limitations, and by which the "powers that be," the united and separated sovereignties, "are ordained of God." A glance at the divine work in forming the American Union in the harmony and distinction of National and State sovereignties, cannot fail to illustrate the subject.

The arrangement, then, of limited supremacy in the central government, and of separate state sovereignties in all but delegated powers, peculiar to the United States of America, is no device of man, no new work of the Philadelphia Convention of 1787, but the marvellous and mysterious work of Providence, then happily accepted. "The powers that be are ordained of God." His overruling Providence settles where the responsibility lies; who are irresponsible. The American arrangement — not our work, but His — has grown out of the Wittenagemot of Britain, a thousand years ago; out of the wisdom of Alfred and the folly of John; out of Anglo-Saxon privileges reclaimed in Magna Charta; out of the Parliaments of Tudors and Stuarts; out of the controversies which prevailed, and the principles and sentiments which were ripening at the settlement of the Anglican New World; out of the House of Burgesses of Virginia, 1619, the first copy of the British Constitution in the West; the first germ of another England in America, in which the people beheld among themselves an image of the British Constitution, which they reverenced as the most perfect model of government;* out of the self-made commonwealth, debarked from the Mayflower at Plymouth, 1620; out of the charters of Massachusetts, Connecticut, and Rhode Island, and the reclamations of unchartered colonies; out of the determination of the States, through all difficulties, to hold the inalienable privileges of Englishmen, to govern themselves on the principles of the British Parliament in each separate colony; and finally, out of the circumstances by which they were wrought at once into method and habits of in-

---

* Bancroft.

dependent action, and into an incipient and growing unity. That they were offsets from England, made them partakers at their departure and in their settlement "of all the rights and privileges of Englishmen;" and that they were planted in the midst of savage tribes prompted by European enemies, made of necessity each Colonial Legislature supreme in the highest act of sovereignty — in war — waiting neither for one another, nor for Great Britain itself. That their exposure was common to all, and that their enemies had a bond of union in their connection with a great European power and by the waters of the West, suggested and required a union practical and substantial, ever progressing towards a unity in form. Each colony became thus another England, and yet all so situated with reference to peace and war as to force the many Englands for common purposes into one. The absolute power of chartered companies or grantees under the Crown, and of the royal Duke himself — the British throne — Parliament — did not, could not, withstand the force of circumstances, the work of Providence, the ordinance of God, preparing separate sovereignties for union in common purposes under a limited supremacy.

As union grew into form, how, from the earliest periods, was State supremacy at once maintained and yielded, until the slow but sure work of Providence produced our actual Union, as expressed in the Constitution! "Danger taught the colonies the necessity of union; and on the first day of May, 1690, New York beheld the momentous example of an American Congress," by the concurrence of other colonies with the proposal of Massachusetts, thus early preparing "the forms of independence and union." *

"The Commissioners at Albany, 1754, were unanimously of opinion that a union of the colonies was necessary for the common defence against the French and Indians." Such, before the Revolutionary struggle, were the germs of union; not of the confederation of 1781, but of the Constitution of 1787; springing up from the original circumstances and condition of the country — from providential direction. As the revolutionary struggle advanced, how, in like manner, were State supremacy and central direction still growing together, and still tending to that distribution of powers of which the Constitution is the literal expression! The actual assembling of

---

* Bancroft.

nine colonies, with the concurrence of others, at New York, October, 1765, and their "agreement on a declaration of rights, and on a statement of grievances;" the general Congress at Philadelphia, September, 1774, the whole uniting in the claim of "free and exclusive power of legislation in their several provincial legislatures," and this in right of emigration, as "free and natural-born subjects" of the "realm of England," and its subsequent acts of sovereignty for the common defence; the imperfect convention acceded to in 1781, retaining too much State sovereignty, and leaving too little with the common head; declining the unity for which Providence had provided of separated sovereignties under a single sovereignty, and thereby requiring its renewal and its establishment; and finally, the actual settlement of the present Constitution in 1787, *not in compromise* of opposing claims, but in *conformity* with the provisions of Nature and Providence, with the ordinance of God; — all these were but so many stages of development according to necessity and circumstances, until the *letter* came to agree with the *substance* — the expression with the reality. The Constitution of the United States was not first made when it was voted and proffered to the people, but then merely unfolded and delivered as the gift of Heaven, which ages had provided. Our fathers, like their fathers, in every stage of their progress, in all their remonstrances and declarations, claimed *not new privileges, but old ones;* not what men could give, but what God had given; brought with them across the Atlantic, and exalting their provincial assemblies into embryo Parliaments; each *new* England holding of right what no king or Parliament could take away. Our fathers, like their fathers, the barons of Runnymede, and the Lords and Commons of later times, said, for substance, *Nolumus leges Angliæ mutari:* What God has given us must not be changed — cannot be changed.

In aid of the progressive circumstances producing the union of separate and sovereign States has been the physical structure of the country, fitted for local governments equally, whether on the narrowest or broadest scale, — for a Virginia and New York, or a Delaware and Rhode Island, — and at the same time enabling and requiring the combination of many into one. The first settlements along the Atlantic border, so widely separate as to be obliged to act alone, found the ocean which washed their shores a bond of union, enabling them to unite for the common defence. As the settlements extended, new bonds of union were found in the rivers and lakes of the North, and then again in the great rivers of the West, joining, almost, the lakes and rivers of the North, and binding all to the southern gulf; connecting the North and the South, the East and the West, as by the ordinances of nature itself, which cannot be changed. And then, as the States have grown stronger under the protection of the Union, how have they employed their protected strength, not in sundering, but in strengthening and increasing the national bonds; the States more capable of separate action because they were united, and employing that action in perfecting and establishing the Union; binding themselves by separate acts of sovereignty more firmly into one! New York building the Erie Canal; Pennsylvania uniting the Delaware and the waters of the West and South; and other States joining them, first in artificial watercourses, and now in railroads, the works of many separate States, overspreading the Union, bind together with new bands the four great quarters of the land into a still more indissoluble one. This view of necessary union, by means of physical condition, matched by a providential work, did not fail of influence in producing the letter of the Constitution, and in securing the formality of ratification. "It has often given me pleasure," says Governor Jay, urging the adoption of the Constitution, in concurrence with Madison and Hamilton, "to observe that independent America was not composed of detached and distinct territories, but that one connected, wide-spreading country was the portion of our western sons of liberty. A succession of navigable waters forms a kind of chain round its borders, as if to bind it together; while the most noble rivers in the world, running at convenient distances, present them with highways for the easy communication of friendly aids, and the mutual transportation and exchange of their various commodities." The effect of internal improvements by the authority of separate and sovereign States, in perfecting and continuing the Union, as the protecting Sovereign of the whole, is thus referred to by Mr. Clay, December 29, 1835, while yet the providential mystery of union, by separation, was but partly developed: —

"The States have undertaken what the general government is prevented from accomplishing. *They are strengthening the Union* by various lines of communication thrown across and through the mountains. New York has completed one great chain; Pennsylvania another, bolder in conception, and far more arduous in execution. Virginia has a similar work in progress, worthy of all her enterprise and energy. A fourth, farther south, where the parts of the Union are too loosely connected, has been projected. These and other similar undertakings completed, we may indulge the patriotic hope that our Union will be bound together by ties and interests that shall render it indissoluble."

Thus far, most certainly, the Constitution is *conformity*, not *compromise*. State supremacy in all but delegated powers, and supremacy at the centre in those powers, is *God's ordinance, and not man's device*, leaving the responsibility for slavery with the States, forbidding it to the United States. The United States are not responsible *under* the Constitution, and are not responsible *for* the Constitution against all scruples and evasions, all pretensions and attempts to the contrary.

CHAPTER IX.

UNION BY SEPARATION.

The work of Providence for a thousand years ; for one hundred and fifty years from the first settlement of this country, decided the American arrangement of State and National sovereignties — the facts, as the Constitution has expressed them in the letter. The force of circumstances, the necessities of our condition, inherited powers growing and developing in the progress of events, made the Constitution for us, not by us, as God's ordinance and not as man's device ; not by compromise, but conformity. The framers of the Constitution had this highest wisdom, that they perceived and expressed what Providence had wrought. All honor to their memory ! This arrangement of Heaven finds illustration in the whole work of the States by which we became the United States above and against all enemies and rivals, and in the harmony of Central and State sovereignties as the United States. If the States had not been separately sovereign, we should never have become the United States at all ; and since we have become such, neither absorption nor separation, neither concentration nor nullification, have been found to be possible.

What, then, is it that has given the United States a place among the nations of the earth, as a great, undivided, and happy people? How is it that the most perfect government of the European world has taken root and grown until it has spread itself almost from gulf to gulf, and from ocean to ocean ? — that a new and larger England has been established in America? that we have another Magna Charta, parliaments, the English race, and language, and character, and principles, and literature, prevailing over all other European claimants, over all enemies and rivals? Is it not due to the separate State sovereignties that we are the United States at all ?

Let it not be forgotten that the early advantage belonged to other nations ; — to France, occupying the northern and southern gulfs, and their tributary rivers, with lines of military posts, and hostile tribes extending two thousand miles in our rear ; to Holland, at the mouth of the Hudson, the most important intermediate inlet, separating the English settlements from each other; to Spain, even, especially when the others were no longer enemies or rivals, taking the place of France on the Gulf of Mexico and the rivers of the West, and with such hope as to establish a New Madrid almost at the mouth of the Ohio, as the future capital of the " Great (Spanish) West." Whence came it that the English race — hemmed in upon the coast of the Atlantic, divided from each other by an intermediate State, shut out from the great inlets and intercourses, and incessantly assailed — so marvellously prevailed over all enemies and rivals ; nay, assimilated to themselves enemies and rivals, and are assimilating all other European nations into one undivided English people? Whence, but because at their beginning each State was a *New* England, with a parliament capable of government and action at every separate point of attack from that hostile array, and of uniting also for the common defence? It was New England, for instance, with all the elements of our actual union, combining the forces of Massachusetts, Rhode Island, Connecticut, and New Hampshire, which secured the surrender of Louisburg, " the Gibraltar of America," June 17th, 1744. It was Virginia, with a constitutional life beating high from 1619, with a virtual sovereignty competent to devise and execute in regard to her Ohio frontier, which held fast to the valley of the west for the united whole, educating thus the " Father of his Country." It was the colonies, separate and combined, chiefly, which secured the surrender of the French posts on the western lakes and rivers, and the cession of Canada, 1760 ; and at length the whole land, from gulf to gulf, to one undivided English people, assimilated from all European nations, to be carried forth as one people, from ocean to ocean. This vast and growing nation, united by separation, more intimately blended into one than any other nation on the face of the globe — woven together by mutual relations and intercourse, as by the minutest threads, into one common, yet divided unity, has been formed by means of separate States, whose principles of life have been the gift of a gracious Providence for a thousand years. We are what we are in the existing fact, because we were what we were in the very elements of our being. The elements of the Constitution made the United States, not the United States the Constitution; have given us our united and have left to us our separate responsibilities.

And how has it been since we have been the United States? Have we been able to set aside the ordinance of God which made us many, and thereby made us one? to be less or more than separate sovereignties under a limited head? Even under the convention of 1781, when we undertook to reverse the appointment of Heaven manifested in that closer union, which "danger" produced as early as 1690, which the necessities of the "common defence" suggested in 1754, and which, against all reluctances of the States, was forced upon Congress and upon Washington, that there might be one mind and action for the whole, in matters pertaining to the whole,— how signally we failed! When common dangers and necessities ceased, we substituted for that powerful bond a rope of sand, that we might become what we had never been from the first, mere separate sovereignties. But did we remain so? Could we thus set aside the unity which Providence had wrought for us, and which He had made the condition of those single sovereignties we claimed? How signally we acknowledged a bond never to be loosed, even when we thought we had refused to be bound at all! Strange to say! That Providence which overrules the governments of men, which sees in the germ that which unfolds itself in the growth, which preserves above and beyond human forethought that which human forethought presumes to destroy, still kept in the minds of our fathers the substantial idea and intention, at the very time they refused the form which His providence required. Claiming to be but thirteen separate States, under rules and methods which rendered united action impossible, they claimed, nevertheless, the reality and the substance of State sovereignties and central supremacy, for then, and for the future; for the original thirteen States and for indefinite increase; for more and still more separate sovereignties, all becoming more and more united under a common head! What else meant they by the motto, adopted June 20th, 1782, "E Pluribus Unum," — many and yet one; one and yet many, above and beyond all powers of division or of concentration, while by the letter of the "convention" they were many and not one? What else meant they by the reverse of that national seal, — by that significant emblem, that devout acknowledgment, — the unfinished pyramid, compact and firm, to become more compact and firm the more stones are added to the structure; and yet not by man's device, but by God's ordinance, under the eye of Heaven, and with the devout acknowledgment, "*Annuit Cœptis*," — God has built the United States, and will build them more and more perfectly in one. At the very time when the States claimed to be many and not one, they acknowledged the indissoluble unity which Providence had wrought.

And since the adoption of the Constitution, — the conforming of the letter to the arrangements of Heaven, — how remarkably has the ordinance of God prevailed, making still the many one, and the one many. The States have not been able to be less or more than self-regulating States, under the protection of a supreme government: — The United States have not been able to be less or more than a supreme government amidst self-regulating and sovereign States. Absorption and separation, concentration and nullification, have been alike impossible.

Thus, in every stage of progress, before and since the Convention of 1787, the Constitution of the United States is God's ordinance and not man's device; the wisdom of its framers is manifest, not in compromising with the will of man, but in conforming to the wisdom of heaven; no less in what is withholden than in what is given, in what remains with the States, than in what is yielded to the confederated head. In the words of Washington, applicable equally to a thousand years of the history of our fathers, and to more than two hundred from the settlement of these States: "Every step by which the United States have advanced to the character of an independent nation seems to have been distinguished by some token of an overruling Providence." * Especially after the British Constitution was transplanted to these States, distinct and separate, and yet forced to both independent and united action; — circumstances, declarations, acknowledgments, customs, precedents, common law, and common understanding, had settled at once State supremacy, and a confederated head, before the Convention of 1787, so that that Convention could not annul either — whose work was not compromise, but conformity to the work of Providence, which they could not overrule. Nay, so absolute was that Providence, so controlling were circumstances and events, that the Convention of 1787 could not have

---

* Inaugural, 1789.

prevented, for substance, the present Constitution. Had they failed to form it, it would have gone on to form itself, developing and fixing the reality in anticipation of the letter. Nay, more; so certain and so determinate is the work of Providence, the ordinance of God, that it cannot now be set aside; not the sovereignty of the States, not the supremacy of the United States. A Convention of 1856 could not annul the great provisions of the Constitution forced upon us three score years ago — could restore neither the separate States nor the United States to the nominal powers and real impotence which followed the peace of 1783 — could not make the United States the seat of power and responsibility for the several parts. Impossible attempt! which, adopted in the form of a new and accepted Constitution, would disappear like the baseless visions of the night, leaving the substance which God has ordained — State sovereignties and limited supremacy, as settled principles of the American, as Magna Charta and the Bill of Rights, are of both it and the British Constitution; as *old and not new* — the inheritance of the past, and not the gift of the present — conformity to Providential arrangement, and not compromise with the will of man. Impossible attempt! to concentrate authority so as to make the United States responsible for what has been the separate work of the States; or so to assume State powers as to set aside the legitimate and prescriptive supremacy of the United States.

And do men dream that they ought to break up what God has thus established without their devices, above their work — to dissolve the Union formed by the Providential fittings and cements of many centuries? Do men dream that they can resolve, and speak out of being, what God has spoken into being, above all counter-plans of their enemies and of themselves — that they can break up that union by which God has provided for the highest prosperity of each several part, and in that prosperity, for a more powerful and wider unity? What if the provisions which God wrought out in a thousand years of English and Colonial history — the work of Divine Providence above and against man; what if these were set aside, as the mere letter which man's hand had written, the mere device and decree of the Philadelphia Convention — would they be set aside? Could they? What if the Union were dissolved by unanimous vote, by peaceable consent, into two Unions, or three, or four, or into thirty sovereign States; would the Union be dissolved?

Could it? Impossible! again and again, impossible! Not thus can man contravene the "powers ordained of God"; not thus destroy in a day, God's work for centuries — not thus break down the pyramid built, and still rising, compact and firm under the eye of the Omnipotent! *Dissolve the Union!* Why, we should still lie bound together by the same waters, the same oceans, and gulfs, and bays, and rivers, and lakes, which God has given us in common; and by the same canals and railroads which, under his ordinances, our hands have built; binding us into an indissoluble one! — bound together by the same necessities, and facilities of mutual intercourse — the same inherited and prescriptive powers of acting separately for separate purposes, and of acting together, for purposes common to all! Dissolve the Union! Why, the Union would return upon us again, as it did when we attempted to dissolve it in 1781 — when we preferred to be parts, and not a whole — would return as it did in 1787 — in the letter of the Constitution.

A Convention of 1856, could it dissolve the Union? The States north of Mason and Dixon's line — the States south of that sectional boundary — under whatever scruples or jealousies, can they recede? Could they dissolve the Union? We venture to say that if a dissolution of the Union should take place, with whatever unanimity of decision or permission, that it would not take place; that it would be as nugatory as the (quasi) dissolution of 1781, which produced the letter of the Constitution. King John and King James may think that they can break up the Providential arrangements which are growing into the British Constitution, that they can make a subservient or a despotic monarchy; but they cannot. The Constitution reappears above them and against them, as the growth of the olden time, in a new Magna Charta, and a new Bill of Rights. The northern States may think they can withdraw from the southern, and thus only be innocent of their errors; the southern may think they can withdraw from the northern, and thus only be safe from their interference; but they cannot put asunder what God has joined together. Above and against them, the Constitution will reappear, and the union of State sovereignties be more and more established.

There is but one exception to this assumption. No doubt separation into two hostile parts is possible, at the sword's point, at the cannon's mouth, along the dividing line. At war, there may be a northern and southern Union ; but as with nations naturally and providentially distinct, the exhaustion of war compels to peace ; with States naturally and providentially connected, it would end in reunion. On two sides of a boundary of blood, we may be for a season two nations, until, wearied and worn out with violence and rapine, we become prepared, not for peace between nations, but for another cycle of Union, as a great national family, — as one great and undivided English people, responsible as a whole for what belongs to the whole, and as parts for what belongs to the parts.

CHAPTER X.

THE LAW OF EQUAL FORCES.

BESIDES the fact that State sovereignty with union only in regard to matters in common, is God's ordinance and not man's device, and that the United States have therefore no authority in regard to slavery; there is this further reason against all common legislation in the matter, that the great Overruler has so ordered the balance of sections, that if we had authority, it would be annulled by a necessary impotence.

Owing to relative weight, to equilibrium of forces, the United States would be incapable of action, could never abolish or regulate slavery, even if they had the authority. Providence has so ordered the condition of these United States, that neither the northern nor southern section can make an availing legislation against the will of the other. The North is as impotent as the South, the South as impotent as the North, by the law of equal forces. Sectional equilibrium must prevent any decisive exercise of a central authority, even if that authority existed. Where there is equal weight in both scales, the scales cannot be turned. Equal sections of the same country have only this alternative, ineffectual and injurious contention, or to agree to differ, — submitting to inaction where there is no power to act.

This equilibrium of sections, this impossibility of action, existed at the formation of the Constitution. Besides the inherited and prescriptive right of the States to manage their local affairs, the relative weight of sections forbade sectional action. There was no power in either scale to turn the balance. The States south of Mason and Dixon's line, and the States north of Mason and Dixon's line, were as nearly even poised as possible, (the minute slaveholding of the North notwithstanding,) and from that sectional balance inaction necessarily followed; useless debate giving place to leaving matters as they were. This inaction was inevitable, save only in whatever points both sections could agree, as for manifest reasons they did upon the foreign slave trade, limited to 1808. It was not compromise, but necessity; it was not a criminal yielding to the will of the South, but a providential equilibrium, which left slavery existing by the Constitution, and would have left it even though the United States had possessed authority in the case, unless equals can be unequals; unless equilibrium can turn the scales.

The same principle has governed, not the action but the inaction of the United States, hitherto, in the admission of new slaveholding States. At every stage the previous sectional balance rendered that admission inevitable, — in each case ineffectual and injurious contention giving way to the necessary agreement to differ. Impossibility of action to the contrary, has preserved and continued the original equilibrium. The tree has only grown on both sides according to its former proportions. The evil may or may not be greater than would have ensued if the non-slaveholding States had had both authority and power to open the whole South to a free African population; but how plainly the new slaveholding States have been admitted into the Union by necessary inaction, by means of previous sectional balance! It was no more possible to rule slavery *out* of Alabama, Mississippi, and Louisiana, than to rule it *into* Indiana, Illinois, and Michigan. The southern territory, especially adapted to the productions and labor of the South, became the natural field for southern emigration, as part and parcel of the actual southern population, *with* slavery, while relative weight assured it to them in the Union, against whatever will or opposition of the North. Nay, if the North had possessed a preponderance in the legislative halls, and could have passed a sectional vote against a large minority, the final result would not have been different; so impossible is it to enforce decrees against the natural course of population, against the habits and prescriptions, against the will and opposition of great sections of a country. The most determined vigilance of a military police, the severest penalties and the most rigorous execution of sectional law against one third or one fourth part of the Union, would have been found ineffectual, and must at length have yielded to the pressure. However this may be, most certainly it would have been impossible to have carried out any law against the natural progress of the South towards the West, while the relative weight of both sections was substantially the same;

— for equal sections to have been any thing else but a balance to each other.

The impossibility ruling at the formation of the Constitution, and ruling since in the increasing number of the States, rules still, and would prevent the action of the United States for the regulation or abolition of southern slavery, by authority, precisely as it would be impossible for the South to impose slavery on the North; for the want of sectional preponderance. As at the formation of the Constitution, the thirteen States were balanced upon Mason and Dixon's line, so that a controlling power was impossible to either section, so are the thirty-one States now balanced as equally upon the actual line which separates the free and slaveholding States. Granting the free States the advantage in numbers, in their homogeneous population, and in the vigor and activity of all classes of the people, the balance of the slaveholding States is found in their command of the great rivers of the West, and in their possession of the great staple of northern manufactures. So nearly equal are the two sections, that any absolute and decisive preponderance of the North is impossible. Even if the Senate were constituted on the same principles as the House of Representatives, and thereby a majority of both houses could be secured, how certain it is that no law of regulation or abolition could or would be enforced against the will and opposition of the South! If the United States had at this moment constitutional authority in the premises, it would be impossible to exercise it, from relative weight, from sectional equilibrium. Like two nations, substantially equal, their alternative would be, unavailing strife, or the agreement to differ. In truth, whether enforced or unenforced, legislation would end in establishing that which it began to remove.

Such being our views of the necessary results of sectional equilibrium, we do not accept the common explanation of the allowance and progress of slavery hitherto, as by compromises between the North and the South, or still worse, by southern domination and northern subserviency. As it was not determinate action, but necessary inaction, which ruled in the allowance of slavery by the Constitution, so it was in fixing the sectional line of 36. 30., and in the "treaty" with Texas. So inevitable was inaction from the previous equilibrium of forces, that if the North had prevailed in either case, by some advantage of the moment, most surely it would not have prevailed. No sectional vote, according to northern views, could have been carried out and enforced against the South. Equilibrium could not have given a final and settled preponderance. The maintenance of slavery at the South and its extension to the southern West, has been due, not to voluntary compromise between the North and South, but to the impossibility of turning an even-balanced scale ; not to neglect or consent on the part of the North, but to necessary inaction ; not to northern weight thrown into the scale, but to southern weight itself keeping the balance even ; not to an overruling South, but to equal impotence of both North and South against each other ; not, in fine, to southern domination and northern subserviency, but to that relative weight which gives no occasion for either.

We do not forget the claim that there should then be no United States at all ; that the North should separate from the South, in order not to be partaker of other men's sins. Not to dwell upon the assumption of the last chapter, that this is not left to our choice, — that the union ordained by the will of Providence cannot be broken by the will of man, — we may confidently assert that if we had the power to separate any member from the body, or to divide the body into two living parts, then there is no conceivable reason for doing so. What if we are so equally balanced that the North cannot control the South, nor the South the North ? What if we cannot decree and enforce, the one section against the will and opposition of the other, and thereby each is left to its own choice and responsibility in matters local and sectional ? May we then form no partnership in any thing, because we cannot become partners in every thing ? May we maintain no relations with men, unless they can be ruled by us in all relations ? May government be common for no purposes without being common for all purposes ? In fine, may not the northern and southern sections, though incapable of ruling each other on the great sectional question, still sail on the same oceans, gulfs, bays, and rivers ; under the protection of the same forts and fleets ; and in the same relations to our own separate States and to other nations, by which the common opportunities are preserved and the common thoroughfares of the world kept open ?

Is there, then, no scope at the South for northern philanthropy ? Undoubtedly there is ; none the less because it must needs be without authority, where no authority exists, and without a decisive weight where an overruling Providence has made the balances even. Authority disclaimed, impotence to overrule acknowledged, and the vain struggle of equal sections finished, there will be the freest scope to whatever northern wisdom and good will. With authority we could do nothing, because we form but an equal section of the Union. Without authority, without power, as ready to check our mistaken earnestness as to rouse the mistaken apathy of our brethren; as ready to learn as to teach, we shall find the whole South open to those fraternal councils from which priceless blessings may be hoped.

Of this hope we have a striking illustration. No doubt any attempt on the part of the North to regulate the cultivation of cotton by a sectional vote, would have failed, if there had been authority, for the want of northern weight adequate to overrule the reluctance and resistance which the interference would have called forth. Nevertheless the weight of the South was no hinderance to northern ingenuity and industry. The necessity of leaving the care of cotton to the cotton-growing States, allowed yet fullest scope to northern invention and manufactures, as great elements of southern prosperity. Who can tell how many times the wealth of the South has been multiplied by the cotton-gin of Whitney, by the looms and the labors of scores of Lowells and Manchesters. Let it not be supposed, in regard to the more important matter of their social condition, to the great principles of moral and political economy, that wise and kind reflection and suggestion will be lost upon the South, if in any degree they shall be found emanating from the North.

CHAPTER XI.

ADVANTAGES OF STATE SUPREMACY.

THERE cannot be a stronger appeal to the South than the claim that, whether by authority or power, by inherited rights or sectional equilibrium, the responsibility is theirs alone. If the North desires to see a remedy for slavery, let it disclaim all intention, let it discard all attempt to overrule, acknowledging its own utter impotence, and ceasing the vain struggle of equal sections. Instead of lightening the sense of responsibility by officious interference, let the whole weight of it be left where it properly belongs, assured that the way will be more open to whatever neighborly and philanthropic aids. In the hope that our suggestions will be as well received as they are well meant, we proceed to note certain direct advantages of our system of State Administration.

1. The slaveholding States, alone, are competent to the specific wisdom and skill required. They, only, can form and apply a Code truly remedial.

It were to deny the principle on which this work proceeds, to assert that wisdom and skill cannot come from without. But no one can feel more sensibly than the writer, that all suggestions from the North must be made with deference to the local knowledge and experience of the South. Whatever wisdom may be supposed to be derived from the whole experience of mankind and the history of races rising in the social state ; or from American experiments with barbarism, and the European problem of the " masses," it can be only in the seed, and not in the harvest, until it has been cultivated and ripened on southern soil. Those, only, who are intimate with the character and condition of the people, and with the climate and productions of the South, are capable of developing completely the principles of well-being, in application to masters and slaves — to the whole southern population.

Besides, how vain were all wisdom, all devices and methods from without, except by coöperation from within, except with aid and scope given on the spot. If the northern philanthropist could proffer the maturity and the fulness of wisdom, he can do nothing unless the southern patriarch adopt and employ it. The wisdom of the cotton-gin would have been useless, if it had not been welcomed and applied by the growers of cotton.

It is well, further, that the responsibility is not even sectional; that the southern section cannot legislate for the southern section as a whole; that each State is separately responsible. Now, any experiment must needs be tried on a small scale, with the opportunity of varying as occasion may require, until it can be made a fit model for the rest; until, commending itself to the common sense and observation of men, it shall claim to be adopted by all. It is well, especally, that the responsibility is not national, and committed to divided councils, incapable of any other action but interminable contention; nay, that it is not committed to a central power, capable of delaying or preventing desirable measures on the one hand, or of forcing those that are undesirable, on the other; or even of carrying with over haste, methods which are practicable only by slow degrees, instead of limited and local experiments, growing at length into a wisdom and skill fitted for the widest adoption.

What we mean here, may be illustrated by a reference to the West Indies — to the changes produced there by a sovereign authority over, and not with them; a legislation for them, and not by them; without local knowledge and experience, and against the good will of the property and influence of the country, and yet of universal effect. The first law — that of apprenticeship, was itself declared over hasty, injudicious, by the subsequent act of emancipation, while that act done and finished, for better or worse, is rather claimed as good *a priori*, from abstract principles, than by the experiment itself; nay, is acknowledged or feared as a failure, by those even who aided and hailed the enactment. How disastrous the forced result may prove, is thus expressed in the London Times, April 30, 1849: "With a race of blacks, new to the enjoyments, and unschooled by the discipline of freedom, it may yet be our fate to see the hopes of benevolent, and the enthusiasm of religious men, destroyed by the hideous spectacle of a new and more barbarous St. Domingo rising on the ruins of the British Antilles." In illustration, if it be not proof, of the downward tendency of the actual emancipation of the British West Indies, we have the statements from Jamaica, that "the poverty and industrial prostration of that island, are almost incredible. Since 1832, out of the six hundred and fifty-three sugar estates then in cultivation, more than one hundred and fifty have been abandoned, and the works broken up. This has thrown out of cultivation over 200,000 acres of land, which in 1832 gave employment to about 30,000 laborers, and yielded over 15.000 hogsheads of sugar, and over 6,000 puncheons of rum. During the same period, over five hundred Coffee plantations have been abandoned, and their works broken up. This threw out of cultivation over 200,000 acres more of land, which in 1832, required the labor of over 30,000." Whether these statements be worthy of credit or not, they serve our present purpose of illustrating what we mean by over hasty and injurious legislation from without, against local knowledge, and the good will of the property and influence of the Slave States themselves.

2. The wisdom of a single State has every opportunity to be extended to other States, with such variations as the peculiar condition of each may require. If the separation of the States gives the fairest field for a safe, unexpensive, and advantageous experiment, their mutual intercourse affords the freest possible scope for its repetition, for its adoption according to its tried and proved merits, as wide as the evil to be remedied. It is well that each State only has the power within itself to devise and to attempt, to vary and to modify, to begin in its weakness and ignorance, and to grow in wisdom and skill by well-meant endeavors, until, by the aid of Him who enables the simple-hearted, it may be found accomplishing the work — and then it is well that the way is open for the example to be followed by other States in like condition. The narrowness of the sovereignty, incompetence everywhere, save within each slaveholding State, gives the best opportunity for the beginning, and the intimate union of the States for the wide and rapid extension of a wise and successful experiment. Happy, in so great a matter as changing the whole condition of society, that no central authority can act upon the great Section concerned — can make an immediate and universal change. Happy, if there may be found one or more among the States competent and concerned, so truly patriarchal as to undertake a method of well-being suited to the peculiar case ; to begin on the

plainest principles of common sense, and to grow in wisdom and skill until it shall become a fit model for the rest. Of the advantage thus stated, we find ample illustration in the general history of human progress, and in the annals of our own nation in particular.

The mechanical and industrial improvements of the age were not over hastily undertaken — were not absolutely hindered by central sovereignties, but grew up from individual devices and experiments, until they had attained a perfection in which they could become the helpers as well as the foster children of many nations. Had they depended upon the Parliament of Great Britain or the Congress of the United States, or still more upon the united councils of all civilized nations which have adopted them, they would not have been so wisely made, or so rapidly and so universally introduced It was the smallness of the sphere, rather, which enabled successful experiment; and when successful experiment was made, it was intimate connection of the parts of a country with each other, and of country with country, which facilitated their ready and general adoption. An experimental Watt, proffering his improvements to the parties concerned for a moiety of the savings above the use of Newcomen's steam engine, brought a "remedy" to all the coal mines of Great Britain; concurring with an experimental Arkwright and Whitney, "reformed" all the cotton fields of the South, all the spinning wheels and looms of Europe and America; and with an experimental Fulton on a single river of a single State in the New World, "emancipated" navigation from the chains of wind and tide, almost in every sea, and lake, and river of the globe.

This last illustration introduces us to the peculiar advantages of our own system, depending as it did, for its first impulse and scope, upon the questionable patronage of a single State. The State of New York, in the use of a power finally decided not to be hers, gave steam navigation to the United States and to mankind. If the final interpretation of the Constitution by the Courts of the Union had been given at the first moment of experiment and uncertainty, it would have hindered instead of advancing; it might have destroyed instead of sustaining, the great undertaking which, besides opening the wide world of waters to regular and rapid communication among men, has also shortened by three fourths, the great thoroughfares by land, through our own States, and almost throughout the world.

The same State of New York, in the use of her unquestionable powers, has given another illustrious example. Without authority over any other State, without power — simply by acting for herself, and proving for herself, and thus showing what was good for others, she has led the whole sisterhood in her train. Not by authority over the Union, but without authority; not by centralization of the States, but by subdivision into separate sovereignties, has been produced a system of internal improvements extending over all the States; and this work of many as one, is due to the enterprise and success of the single State of New York, in undertaking and carrying through, the Erie Canal; becoming thus, in the best sense, the *Empire State*, ruling by not ruling, becoming by example and influence alone, the welcomed Sovereign of the whole. A single State, in the use of its own inherited and acknowledged powers, experimenting upon its own facilities and resources, with great misgivings, devised, attempted, modified, perfected, the first great work of Internal improvement; and behold other States have followed her example, until all are bound together by Canals and Railroads, doing the work of each separate State for its own behoof, and yet binding all into an indissoluble one; all becoming more firmly united by being so distinctly divided; a more perfect one because they were many.

This capacity in a State, not to rule many States, a whole section, or the whole Union, but to influence by a worthy example, has illustration in our earlier annals; in the rise and progress of the separate States and of the Union, which at length became established and completed. The whole course of events shows the advantage to the whole of separate Sovereignty in the parts. For its own all-important purposes, we honor and value the United Sovereignty which God has given us; but in so far as we desire either a sectional or general result in regard to purposes belonging to the separate States, we accept rather the opportunity and the scope for *influence* which has prevailed so often, and wrought out the needful advantage. By the influence of State upon State, we have become what we are. From the beginning it has been each separate State, experimenting unconsciously for other States, which has led forward our deliverances and our blessings. In the wars with the savage tribes, and their European abettors and leaders, and with the mother country, and in the rise and progress of our separate and united powers, up to the Constitution itself; advantages have grown by means of our separate Sovereignties; State example and influence, prompting, directing, and uniting different Sections, and the whole. A few examples will suffice.

It was, then, by this influence of State upon State, that the Revolution of 1688 was carried through the American Colonies. In the acknowledgment of William and Mary, and the establishment of the "Bill of Rights," says the historian Bancroft, "a popular insurrection beginning at Boston, extended to the Chesapeake and the wilderness." The idea of an American Congress succeeded naturally thereupon. "Invitations were given by letter from the General Court of Massachusetts, and extended to all the Colonies, as far at least as Maryland. Massachusetts, the parent of so many States, is certainly the parent of the American Union," born in truth of the influence of State upon State, on the first day of May, 1690, when "Congress" met at New York. That great change in the future of all the States — in their prospective unity as an English people, with the first principles of the British Constitution, strengthening State Governments, and uniting them for the common good — the capture of Louisburg by Gov. Shirley in the year 1745, was due to the action of Massachusetts — to the influence of Massachusetts upon the sisterhood of Colonies. " The Legislature of Massachusetts, after some hesitation, resolved on the expedition by a majority of a single vote. New York and Pennsylvania sent a small supply of artillery and provisions. New England alone furnished men."

The grand coalition (for so it may be called,) which delivered the British Colonies forever from "the French and Indians," — which developed them into (almost) independent States, while it combined them (almost) into a Sovereign Unity, was due to the action of Virginia in sending Major Washington "to insist on the evacuation of the French Posts on the Ohio," and in their raising troops to assert their rights; inspiring thus all the Colonies with a sense of their separate powers, and of the necessity and advantage of Union, and giving rise to the *quasi* Union at Albany in 1754. The influence of Virginia through a long course of exertions and deliverances, brought the French war to a prosperous conclusion, and established the British race and influence in North America; to grow how soon, and how flourishing, into the United States! The resolutions of Patrick Henry in the Legislature of Virginia — the circular letter of Massachusetts proposing to call a central Congress, produced the meeting of nine Colonies at New York, with the concurrence of the rest, on the 2d Tuesday of October, 1765. The proposition of Massachusetts during the exile of its Legislature to Salem, for a Continental Congress, by its influence, produced the General Congress of September, 1774, and the Declaration of Rights, claiming all the privileges of British subjects for the American States ; and, in truth, the Declaration of Independence itself, July 4, 1776, and its effective and triumphant accomplishment. And finally, the proposition of Virginia for the Convention of 1787, influenced all the States to join in forming the Constitution, which, in essence, the course of events had wrought out — in completing and crowning the work which had grown so long by the interaction of the States upon one another, in the perfect unity of separated Sovereignties, indissolubly one, and yet capable of indefinite increase.

This history of the influence of State upon State must not be dismissed without referring also to the individual influence which is at the same time exemplified for the encouragement of the philanthropist and patriarch. Each State movement was but the movement, extended and multiplied, of patriotic individuals, acting with the Providence, and aided by the Providence, which has been with these States for good. Especially may the crowning work, the adoption of the Constitution, and its favorable operation, be ascribed not to the central authority or power of either the Congress or Convention of 1787 ; but in how great a degree to the influence of Washington, and other leading patriots, in forming the Constitution ; and then to the illustrious *three* who united in defending and commending the instrument, in forming which two of them had part. The essays of *Publius!* who can tell their influence in securing the adoption of the Constitution, and its favorable operation for more than three score years ? The numbers of the *Federalist*, the joint work of Jay, Hamilton, and Madison ; without authority, without power — ruled without ruling — still rule, and will not cease to rule the American States.

It is not authority, then, nor power of the whole over the parts, nor overruling force, nor the weight of Section against Section, to which we are taught to look, for whatever, through this wide domain it is desirable to accomplish, but to *influence*, which any State may exert upon many States ; nay, any individual, if indeed he may find and bring forth wisdom for the people. The whole voice of American history demands that each separate State, or any portion of the States, shall be strong over the rest by influence alone. Northern philanthropy will do its utmost — not by authority where no authority exists — not by power where there is no power — not by an imperative balance where there is an essential equipoise; but without authority and power, and notwithstanding impotence, whenever it shall unite an available wisdom to fraternal good-will.

It is thus with moral as with physical forces. We take account of *vis inertiæ* as well as *vis:* of impotence as well as power, whether that power may not contend idly against its bounds, or that it may be accumulated and applied — of the mountain sides, up which the river cannot run, as well as of its natural flow — of the banks which protect the valley, as well as of the stream which waters it and bears its products on its bosom — of the rocky barriers which hold back internal oceans, and preserve half a continent from the flood of waters, as well as of the tremendous torrent. Nay, instead of contending with a *vis inertiæ* which we cannot annul, we make a new power out of impotence itself. The attempt to send the current up the mountain side would be in vain; the rocky barrier removed, there would be only desolation and ruin; but the dyke rightly interposed, and behold the river fertilizes the country, or does the labor of thousands of men. What if there be impotence in the United States, which forbids their action? Out of that very impotence may come the most effectual strength. Who shall tell us that when the impotence is acknowledged, it will not itself prove the very reservoir of power? that when we shall have left off the vain attempt to make the waters run up the hill, we may not find a method of raising and directing the fertilizing and working floods? Out of the United States " cannot," against which we have wrought and struggled in vain, what a "can" might grow, working wonders of blessing for the North and the South.

CHAPTER XII.

THE COMMON TERRITORIES AND FREE SOIL.

WHAT are the rights and duties of the United States, as to the common territories? Ought they to claim them?—Can they secure them by a sectional vote as FREE SOIL, as excluding slavery forever? In answering these questions, we assert, *first, the right of the South to carry their property and labor, in the forms existing in the progress and establishment of our political Union, into their fair proportion of whatever territory is, or may be, the common property of all.*

Of course we mean their political right; their right relatively to the United States; their right of doing, as opposed to our right of hindering, independently of the moral question, in regard to which they are responsible to God and not to the United States. Politically, relatively, so far as our right of control is concerned, the slave states have the right, not only to retain slavery if they will, but to carry it, as it was at the time of the completed union, into their equitable proportion of any territory we may hold in common; and those States must be held accountable if they take advantage of a political right to perpetuate a moral wrong. But whatever wrong they may choose to commit within the old and settled prescription, we (the United States) have no political right to forbid or prevent.

The right thus stated, is plain on the general principles of partnership. The rights of partnership extend to all property held or acquired in common, and do not leave the question of individual application and use to be judged and settled according to the conscience or will of the stronger party. If in a mercantile partnership of three, one of the parties were found disposed to invest his share of the profits in the slave trade itself, the other two would have no right to withhold his dividend. Their only course would be to pay over to their erring brother his own, and then, as individuals, to do what might belong to them as individuals, in dissuading him from the error. In our political partnership we have an instance in point. The surplus revenue was property in common, and as such, belonged equally to all the States. Did any one ever dream that the surplus revenue was liable to be withheld from the South, except on the condition that none of it should be employed in the purchase of slaves? or even in that crying abomination, the purchase of families torn asunder? What if the distribution of the surplus revenue to the South might enable the purchase of thousands of slaves in the worst form of the traffic, had the United States any right to withhold the southern dividend?

What is plain in a mercantile partnership, what is plain in the partnership of the States as to funds in common, is not less plain as to territory in common. In the absence of any specific provision, the principle would hold, that being possessed or acquired in common, it would be to be used in common, according to the custom of the partners at the time of the compact, and continued until now. If it be said that the acquisition of territorial property was not contemplated in the rise and settlement of the Union, — in the articles of partnership, — it may be replied with equal truth, neither was a surplus revenue contemplated; but want of foresight did not change the principles on which the common funds were to be distributed — did not give the right of control or appropriation to the free States — does not give the right of control or appropriation of territory any more than of funds. In either case, also, how plain it is that if the emergency had been foreseen it would have been especially provided for. The presumption that a guaranty of rights in partnership would have been required if the claims had been foreseen, sets aside those claims from all place in the idea of the original contract.

Besides this plain application of general principles, there is not wanting the allowance of the right in question by the Constitution itself; as it seems to us expressed, but most certainly implied. The requirement of the Constitution, " that nothing in it shall be so construed as to prejudice any claims of the United States or any particular State," must, from its very terms, be applicable to territorial as well as other possessions; to surplus lands as well as surplus revenues. How much stronger, then, is the allowance of State claims according to the settled usages of the States when the Constitution was formed, by the immediate connection of the cautionary clause with the very article which asserts the "power of Congress to dispose of, and make all needful rules and regulations respecting the territory or other property belonging to the United States." The northern States are not to be prejudiced, individually or collectively, in the right to their "West," for their capital and labor, for their customs and institutions, i. e., *without* slavery; and if the southern States were the stronger in votes and power, they would have no right by the Constitution to introduce slavery into the northern territories. In like manner, the southern States are not to be prejudiced in the right to *their* capital and labor, for *their* customs and institutions, existing when the Constitution was formed, i. e., *with* slavery. So far as political rights are concerned; so far as regards the relations of each separate State to the United States, as a central sovereignty under the Constitution, the way must be considered equally open for the removal westward of capital and labor; for the North without, for the South with, slavery.

And this right is not asserted merely in behalf of the masters; it is claimed also for the slaves. We have something to propose for them better, as we think, than slavery as it is; but whatever is proposed, whether amelioration or emancipation, we insist that the way shall be open for them to live by their labor; and that the territorial scope on which both northern and southern labor have thriven hitherto shall not be denied to the slaves and the African race. They have the right to claim that their way of support shall not be shut against them — that they shall not be denied the best opportunities of profitable toil. If, as is alleged, slave labor has become unprofitable in any of the States, then have the slaves themselves an interest in other fields where labor may be profitable — where they may live by their labor.

2. But besides the right of the South, we assert further, *the impotence of the United States to enforce any sectional prohibition of the North against the South.* If we will not allow the political right of the South to their equitable share of the common territory, and to its unrestricted use, we have then to find that we cannot set it aside. Whatever the United States may undertake by northern preponderance against the political rights of the South, must fail, for the want of a sufficient northern preponderance — must fail from the equilibrium of forces. As impotent as we should be to regulate

ᴜ abolish slavery in the States, so impotent are we to prevent its removal to the southern "West." If we had the right as partners —if we had the constitutional authority, we have not the decisive power. The great Overruler has so overruled that we cannot rule —has so evenly balanced us that we cannot turn the scale.

No doubt this assertion, this indispensable admission, may be unpalatable, if indeed we wish to overrule; no doubt it may be questioned, because it is unpalatable. But is not the admission indispensable? It may seem easy, at first thought, to make out a case in favor of the North, strong in its homogeneous and active population, its majorities attained in the house of representatives, and at length in the senate also, and we may over-hastily say we can:—the northern section has such preponderance that it can enforce a sectional law excluding the South from territories otherwise open; i. e. *with* slavery as existing at the formation of the Constitution.

Let it be supposed, then, that there are territories otherwise open to slavery, and that we carry our northern will against the will of the South ; that the grand question absorbing all other questions, is at length decided according to the will of the North, and that FREE SOIL is decreed for all present and future territory. Will any man think that the question would thereby be decided? — that that decree could stand? Would the question be settled forever by that minute majority which alone it is possible to suppose? — by that minute preponderance which turned the scale? What if there be a majority in the house? — what if there has come to be a majority in the senate also, and the equilibrium hitherto preserved be technically destroyed? — does that prevent the substantial equilibrium which the great Overruler has put beyond and above the decrees of man? Does that prevent the equipoise still secured by compounded if not simple "ratios?" Does that destroy the weight which the South possesses in its numbers and advantages united? In that substantial equilibrium which Providence has settled, can there be found a settled and decisive preponderance? Will not, must not such a vote as we have supposed be speedily reversed, or become a dead letter by being unenforced? — still showing in the future that equilibrium cannot overbalance.

But suppose the attempt to enforce as earnest, as determined, as rigid as to enact the sectional law ; while yet the South would not obey the law without enforcement. How long would the North persist against the South? How long carry on the almost equal struggle, before it would learn the lesson of equal forces on which we now insist? Or, if the North should persist, determinedly, violently, at the point of the sword, to carry a measure which God has given them no right or power to carry, how long before the South, almost if not quite equal to the North, would be reduced to that quiet submission which would settle the question? — how long before they would become dependants instead of partners, — subject States instead of coequal sovereignties, — before sectional preponderance would take the place of sectional equilibrium? Rather, how long would it be before the wisdom demanded by the actual equilibrium (not compromise, but conformity to an overruling Providence) would rise, and close the useless, baneful strife?

Assuredly, no decree of the United States can be permanent, which is absolutely sectional, — which is made by a casual preponderance, where, in the main, the balances are even. The abolition of the slave trade in 1808, was not carried against the South and over the South, but with and for the South, and therefore it has been permanent and abiding.

This impossibility of decisive action of Section against Section, is no doubt as applicable to any attempts of the South against the North, as of the North against the South. If the North has to learn that it cannot work its sectional will against the unalterable principles of equipoise, so also has the South. The rendition of fugitive slaves was settled by the Constitution, thus far by the consent of the North, that those " held to labor " should not be " discharged," but " delivered up on the claim of the party to whom labor might be due," and no doubt this settlement may remain fixed, so long as the South shall insist only on the delivery, on proof, before and by the proper authorities. But suppose the South to require more, — action without proof — " delivery " before decision that " service and labor were due," and the coöperation of citizens, under severe penalties, against the general will and feeling of the North; can such a sectional law be enforced? Can it be other than a dead letter, or the occasion of baneful, endless contention for the want of any sufficient southern preponderance?

What, then, it may be asked, is to be the issue, as it regards southern institutions and all the interests of property connected therewith? Is mere equipoise to be as fatal as northern preponderance? Is southern "property" to become worthless by southern impotence, in the even-balanced scale? By no means: impotence acknowledged, new powers may arise out of that very impotence itself. There is a better "cordon" by which slave property may be at once retained and enhanced, than any Fugitive Slave law, — needing no *posse comitatus*, no fines, imprisonments, or blood. There is a method, dimly seen in the confusion of the times, in which the North and the South may earnestly concur — a Remedial Code, — an ameliorated slavery, under which those "held to labor" shall not wish to escape, and the northern philanthropist shall have no wish to tempt or aid; making the "cordon" of comfortable livelihood, unbroken families, and happy homes. The time may come when the "being held to service" shall be considered well compensated by the rations and privileges which are its proper counterpart; when free blacks themselves will desire the position of slaves rather than freemen. So long as their condition must be servile and dependent, the well-endowed slave will not think himself below but above the ill-provided freeman.

3. *An absolute free soil is not the desideratum for southwestern territory;* i. e., for Africans in the actual southern proportions to the European race. Without political right, without decisive and overruling power, we could not establish an absolute free soil if we would. What we now assert is, we would not if we could.

This assertion is not made against but for the African race; not to prevent, but to secure their well-being. We have not claimed free soil for the slave States themselves, and we cannot, therefore, for any territories whose ratio of races is to be the same. No doubt the claim of the African race to the "pursuit of happiness" is equal to that of the European; but in so far as that claim is on us, it is that we should help and not hinder that pursuit. In so far as depends on us, they are not to be endowed with "too free a freedom," lest they be thereby "less free," and some of their present bonds are to be retained, if they may thereby be "more free."

Free Soil, indeed! The two races belting the continent from the Atlantic to the Pacific, all States and all territories in their present actual Southern proportions; the European, with all the advantages of skill and capital, and crowding labor, too; the African advanced, indeed, but how little, comparatively, beyond the barbarism of his fathers and his cotemporaries in Africa; without skill, and enterprise, and energy, and capital, and amidst the crowding laborers of Europe —— will any law of free soil make free soil to the African race? Will it assure the protection and direction of capital in aid of African labor, or of African labor in aid of capital? May it not hinder and obstruct, in place of helping the pursuit of happiness? If by free soil be intended an American or even a British freedom; the whole history and condition of the African race, their aboriginal barbarism, and their present state and relations, may be supposed to cry out against it. Bonds are needful to make free. Let all good bonds be retained, whether on the slave or the master; let bad bonds only be loosed. No matter for the name. Free soil, in name, cannot make the thing, the substance, the reality. Slavery, with its bad bonds loosed, its good bonds retained, cannot prevent the well-being of the race. No matter for the name. Let it be slavery ameliorated, or freedom restricted up to the truest well-being of capital and labor, of European and African, and then the two races may flow together in their southern proportions, over the southern "West," with equal opportunity for the "pursuit of happiness."

This claim for an ameliorated slavery, or a restricted freedom in the Territories, proceeds on the supposition that the demand for free soil is indeed in behalf of the African race, and not against them; that it is not the ban of exclusion from the climates and employments to which their long settlement in the New World has given them a title. But is it so? or do the advocates of free soil intend the boon for the European alone, to the exclusion of the African? Is it in truth intended to admit the negro in southern proportions, with the full franchises of the North? And does this united cry prove its sincerity, by the readiness of the States from which it comes to make their own soil free? Or is there a common and universal consent, that in the States, free soil in southern ratios cannot, must not be admitted? What answer is made by the free States themselves, amidst their loudest cries, their most determined action for free soil? Are they ready to receive a free African population, in the proportion of one third or one half, to an equal share of social, civil, and political rights? Is New York? Is Pennsylvania? Is Ohio? Indiana? Illinois? Michigan? Are they ready to share their several States with the African race in southern proportions? If the question were now before their own legislatures, of making these States free soil, would they open their doors gladly for one third or one half of their present population to go out, and for an equal number of the African race to come in as fellow citizens and voters, as "the sovereign people" equally with themselves? On the other hand who does not know, that if there were such a population ready to rush in, laws would be instantly made to check the immigration, and to limit the freedom of the immigrants? Massachusetts herself, with her full African franchise, her free soil for her eight thousand of African blood, — would she be "free soil" if the prospect were that in ten years one third or one half of her population would be free negroes, having, like the one hundredth now, their equal share in giving direction to her whole condition; to her industry, and education, and morals, and religion? Would Massachusetts be free soil with this prospect before her? Would her legislature be agreed in continuing and establishing free soil. And if the question before Congress could involve the destinies of Massachusetts, and were about to introduce into her bosom the southern proportion of the African race, making one third, or one half, instead of one hundredth, would her course in Congress still be as hitherto? Would her delegation vote for an absolute free soil? Would her legislature so instruct and advise her representatives and senators?

In truth, whatever lapse of sound judgment there may be in the heat of controversy, and in regard to others and the distant, it may be asserted as the sense of the country, — of the North as well as the South, — that the African race, inheriting barbarism, and but partially civilized; comparatively without capital and skill, and not homogeneous with the leading race, would not, in large proportions, promote the prosperity of a State, or even of themselves, as coequal citizens; that both for their own good and the good of the whole people, they need to be legislated for, rather than to be co-legislators. The sense of the North itself is against free soil. The sense of Massachusetts is against free soil. We do not complain at the reluctance of the North to a large free African population, — to that sense of the necessities of the case which has ruled hitherto, and would rule with still more vigilance in view of any large increase. All that we require is, that all restriction shall wisely seek the well-being of both classes of the people, and that there shall be a corresponding mitigation of the northern claim for southern **free** soil : that it shall be temperate, and regulated by the general sense which long experience has produced, and that an ameliorated slavery or a restricted freedom shall be allowed, not as the white man's privilege of oppression, but as the black man's boon — the true method of his well-being.

The points, whether of amelioration or restriction, cannot now be indicated. Keeping in view the general idea of " good bonds retained and bad bonds loosed," the way is open for northern philanthropists and southern patriarchs to unite in the high work of promoting the well-being of both classes and of the whole people. Instead of excluding the Africans of the South from the southern " West," hemming them within their present boundaries, for fear of them as free citizens on the one hand, or dread of slavery as it is on the other; let patriarchs and philanthropists inquire whether there are not principles of justice and mercy, in which the North and the South can agree; whether a Territorial Commission, composed of the sages and patriots of both sections, might not unite with reference to any southern territory, in measures of advantage to both races and to the whole country ; might not speed the natural flow of both races into the great southern " West," with only this condition, that it " shall carry no 'elements of misery which a wise benevolence can cast off," and all elements of well-being which a wise benevolence can carry.

Whatever might be the specific work of such a Commission, the United States would have the same opportunity of influence which we have suggested with reference to an experiment by any State, with some advantages. The vain strife of equal sections laid aside, and the sages and patriots of both sections united in the simple attempt to aid the " pursuit of happiness " by both races, according to their several conditions and character, a general welcome would be prepared for any well-tried and well-proved method, and that method might be aided and hastened by the liberality of the United States. If the ameliorations proposed should be thought to the disadvantage of the slaveholders, the United States are competent to give donations in land to those who may adopt their proposals in regard to an experimental territory. Who shall tell us that when the North and the South shall unite in what they can do, that they will not then be able to do much ; that out of impossibility of action section against section, there may not proceed action by agreement for the highest well-being of the African race, in and with the highest well-being of the whole people? An experimental territory, encouraged by a "land bounty," might be found the most prosperous of territories, if its only bonds upon master and servant were those which make "more free;" might first relieve the South of any surplus African population, and then, reacting on the sources from which it proceeded, might produce and secure the well-being of the sovereign States themselves, in the manner best suited to the condition and character of both classes of their people.

I cannot close this chapter better than by referring to the oft-repeated phrase, prominent in the discussion of the territorial question, and assumed as deciding in favor of Free Soil, in the popular sense of that term — "There is a higher law than the Constitution regulating our authority over the public domain." Undoubtedly there is. Nothing could be more false and fatal than the denial of the "higher law," if thereby be meant, that the laws of Heaven may be transgressed in obedience to the laws of earth; that nations may rightfully do wrong, under their own special provisions for wrong-doing. True! a thousand times true. There is a higher law than the Constitution. All honor to the senator who uttered and urged a principle so high and holy in the Senate of the United States. May it never be forgotten or disobeyed!

But with reference to the legislation to which it was applied by the distinguished senator, what if the higher law forbid, instead of commanding it? What if the great Overruler has given no political right to the United States, to legislate in the matter at all; and has, besides, so evenly balanced them, section against section, that they could not use the right if it had been given? What if the higher law so ruled in the birth, growth, and union of these States, as to give certain rights to the separate States, and to withhold them from the United States; and so ordered sectional arrangements as to produce a substantial equilibrium between the North and the South, proved in every attempt to disturb the balance for more than sixty years? Surely the higher law hitherto has restrained authority, forbidden power "over the domain;" has set limits which could not be passed, leaving free scope only to whatever wisdom and good will.

In like manner there is, undoubtedly, *a higher law than the law of nations.* And yet that "higher law," instead of making every nation's duties the duties of every other nation, or the duties of the parts the common duties of the whole, is found to restrict authority and power to each one's appropriate domain, as the great Overruler has distributed them. Thus, the United States, France, Russia, have nothing to forbid and nothing to allow in regard to miserable Ireland; nothing to do in its behalf, save only what no "law of nations," no "balance of power" can forbid or hinder, — the work of heavenly charity.

And this work of heavenly charity, — free to every nation on the face of the earth, — is not restrained from any part of our beloved country, by any barriers which Heaven has ordained. There is free scope, notwithstanding; nay, there is free scope, thereby, for the utmost wisdom and good will. True, there is a law higher than the Constitution, ruling the Constitution itself, withholding as well as giving political rights, withholding as well as giving political power, forbidding sectional overruling as surely as beach and rock forbid the ocean to overrule the land, and as surely with kind and merciful intent. Do not tell us that a "higher law" requires the sea to go farther than to its appointed bars and doors, its "proud waves," not to be stayed, so that it may flood the world with good. Rather let the sea obey the law which restrains it, and remain shut up in its "decreed place," for then only shall it be the never-failing source of dew, and rain, and fountain, and river, and lake, for a blessing to all people and all times.

CHAPTER XIII.

SUGGESTIONS FOR A REMEDIAL CODE.

KEEPING in view the principles illustrated in the preceding chapters, the leading points of a REMEDIAL CODE are suggested in the following sections, in their bearing upon the well-being of both masters and slaves. This is done, not in the view of preparing them for freedom, — of any " apprenticeship," whether shorter or longer, — but on the supposition of a continued and abiding relation, in the full assurance that the evils and woes of slavery are not of its essence, and that its advantages and blessings may therefore be retained and cherished by a Christian State.

The suggestions for a remedial Code are made with great diffidence. The writer is deeply sensible how difficult it must prove to match the peculiarities of condition and relation, of race, habit, and position; and especially how imperfect his own suggestions are likely to be without the intimate and special knowledge which he does not possess. And yet he makes them earnestly and hopefully, believing that the most imperfect attempt in the right line is better than mere " pro-slavery," or mere " anti-slavery," and even that diffident suggestions may prove better than any confident and premature completeness.

The great principles of a Remedial Code are sufficiently plain. They dawn in the words of Mr. Pitt, anticipating the abolition of the slave trade: " They " (the slaves) " might be relieved from every thing harsh and severe, and put under the protection of the law ; " and of Mr. Wilberforce, " Under the protection of the law is in fact to be a freeman." Indeed they appear again and again, and still more and more clearly, in propositions and recommendations from the slaveholding States themselves, giving assurance that kindly suggestions from whatever quarter will not be in vain, however imperfect they may be. Here, as every where, we must begin in order to learn, — experience must correct unavoidable errors, and unfold and ripen the methods which shall grow into practicable rules. The first thing is to take the right direction, to aim at the right end. This done, every step will be progressive and advantageous.

Section I.

Mutual Bonds of Labor and Capital.

The present relations of master and slave, as it respects labor and maintenance, require to be retained. Fixed providentially together by whatever fault of their predecessors, they are actually in a state of mutual dependence, — the masters for labor, and the slaves for provision; and bonds upon both parties are required for the well-being of both; — not less of the slave than the master, not less of the master than the slave; not less of those depending on labor paid for by capital, than of the capitalists themselves. Those are good bonds which require the master to provide for those dependent on him for their daily maintenance, and for their support in infancy, sickness, and old age, — which enslave him to his slaves; and those are good bonds, also, which require for the master the labor which alone can enable him to make this constant and permanent provision — which enslave them to their master. In the existing condition of the parties, there must needs be "rations" and securities for the laborers and their natural dependents, — and labor, also, in order to rations and securities. The masters must be masters still; must furnish employment, must require labor, that they may provide for want. The slaves must be slaves still, in so far as to render that labor by which alone want can be supplied. "The being held to labor," and the necessary correlative, the being held to maintain labor, are *the essential elements of slavery*, and whatever evils and disabilities are not indispensable to this, *are not of its essence;* are excrescences which humanity and Christianity are required to remove with all possible care and diligence.

The bonds to labor and to maintain labor, thus allowed and required, were, as we have asserted, inconsiderately removed in Europe, and the "masses" have suffered for centuries, from an inconsiderate and unprovided freedom to the serfs. They are even more needful to be retained here with a race not homogeneous, and inheriting more barbarism, indolence, and improvidence.*

In retaining the bonds to labor and provision, there must needs be a benevolent wisdom. The relations of labor and provision must be carefully defined, and the best interests of master and slave equally secured. Whatever has been found to be the amount of labor needful to enable the master to maintain the slave, and the "rations" and privileges to correspond, must be defined. The masters are entitled to the use of their capital, and to some due return for their supervision and direction, as truly as the capitalists of the North, both for themselves and that they may be able to furnish to the slaves an available labor. The slaves are entitled to such avails as labor can permanently secure. "The laborer is worthy of his hire," and must and should be sustained by his labor.

As to the amount to be furnished by the employer, there has been found in the freest States no absolute rule, and wages are necessarily left to take their natural course: falling when they rise so high that capital is compelled to withdraw employment, and rising when prosperous capital seeks to increase the number of its laborers. Under the system of slavery, the rightful "hire" must be for substance on the same principle, viz., *what capital can vay*. The amount of "rations" and privileges must be such that the masters can furnish them, instead of being compelled to cut them off altogether or in part; and such, also, as to give fair encouragement of their being used to good and useful purposes.

Whatever other legislation may be needed in regard to capital and labor, this at least is required, viz., *That the substitution of free for slave labor shall be discountenanced and even disallowed.* The free inhabitants of the slave States are not, of course, to be hindered from labor. But there must be no general admission of immigrant labor, and if it threaten large increase, it must be forbidden. Slave labor must be protected. Those who assert that slavery is to be abolished by substituting free laborers from Europe and Asia, know not what they say. Granted that free labor would be more profitable than slave labor, and that the substitution of it would result in the voluntary emancipation of the slaves, then must the State inter-

* See Chapter VI.

pose, and forbid a change which would take the bread from the mouth of one third or one half of its people ; which would give but the franchise of want and misery. The masters must not have power to substitute emigrant labor, to the loss and damage of the slaves, whatever direct advantage may tempt to the injustice.* Alas for " Africa in America," if they do !

On the other hand, labor must be secured to the masters from the slaves. The masters must have the right to require labor in return for the rations and securities which can be provided by labor alone. The " hire " has its claim upon the laborer. If the master's powers have not been properly defined and checked hitherto, or if custom has permitted abuses of those powers, let whatever needful provisions be made for the future ; but let not their rightful claim be denied or made vain ; let not the system which " holds to labor " be hindered or broken up. Let it remain, as the best means of providing for want, and the best preventive against idleness, improvidence, and vagrancy.

But bonds cannot be retained unless they may be enforced. It belongs, therefore, to a Remedial Code to retain and improve methods of enforcement, whether of " rations " and privileges on the part of the masters, or of labor on the part of the slaves.

First, as to the masters. So far as custom long settled and circumstances secure their due care of their slaves, it is well. But so far as needful, that care must be secured by new legislation, and

---

* Says Mr. Sawtelle, writing from New Orleans, April, 1847, (see New York Observer, July 24,) " The thousands and tens of thousands of the Irish and Germans that have poured in here from the Old World, and which are seen every where rolling cotton bales or hogsheads of sugar, driving hacks and drays, and firing their engines, and actually supplanting the blacks in many departments of labor, are settling the question beyond all controversy, that slavery is not only an unnecessary evil but a pecuniary curse." " I can make more money off my plantation," says one of the largest sugar planters in Louisiana, " by cutting it into small farms, erecting little cottages, and renting them to these families of emigrants, they bringing to my sugar house so much cane annually for rent, thus relieving me from all the vexations, responsibilities, and expenses of providing for a hundred and fifty slaves that must be fed, clothed, and taken care of when sick, whether the crops fail or not; and the time is not far off when the experiment will be made to the entire satisfaction of every southern man ; thereby rendering slaves a pecuniary burden too grievous to be borne, and which must be thrown off."

must be enforced by the executive powers of the State; and so much the more decidedly as the slaves are less able to secure their own rights. Some officer from among the slaves may be the channel of complaint, and some court of redress may issue the complaint without cost to the slave; save where his proceeding shall have been merely vexatious and causeless. The masters, if needful, may be compelled to furnish suitable rations and privileges.

As to the slaves, also, there must needs be means and methods of enforcement. In every country, in the freest States, it is right that labor should be enforced. The State, responsible to provide for pauperism, may take measures to prevent it; may insist on some honest method of supplying the wants of the people; may correct as well as prevent, may prevent as well as correct, idleness, vagrancy and improvidence. If slavery be retained under some ameliorating code, then not only may the masters be compelled to provide rations and securities, but the slaves may be compelled to suitable labor — the labor needful to enable those rations and securities.

Before suggesting the proper methods of enforcing labor, let it first be required that every pains should be taken to prevent the necessity of enforcement — to secure voluntary labor. This will be partially done by retaining slavery, i. e., by keeping up the habits and expectations of those who, from generation to generation, have been " held to labor." Let no formal emancipation hazard those habits and expectations; for, whatever nominal or real freedom might result from it, there can be no release to the mass of men from the labor by which they must live, — from the " sweat of the brow," in which they must " eat their bread," — while yet the old habits and expectations might be broken up without any sufficient substitutes. Let, then, slavery be so far retained as to preserve the old habits and expectations of labor, and the old sentiment of obedience in it, that there may be no lack of the old rations and privileges furnished thereby. It is, I believe, an undisputed fact, that the British West Indies were, in this respect, made too free, — were released unhappily from the habits and expectations of labor — from the sentiment of obedient labor; emancipated, so far as this matter is concerned, to their own disadvantage. If to the old habits and expectations there be added such ameliorations as sensibly promote the well-being of the slaves, there will be every reason to hope for voluntary labor; for which, also, there are these natural provisions , —

1. Task work ; giving at once the needful security to the master for the services due for rations and privileges, and to the slave an opportunity to provide for his comfort beyond those rations and privileges.

Where definite daily tasks are not practicable, *results* may be taken instead; in common parlance, labor may be done by the job; as a field cultivated, a harvest secured, wood cut and hauled, — whether by one, or by a company united under one leading and responsible head.   This method might be carried into any kind of employment, and to any extent within the scope of African contractors, receiving a good margin for their private advantage, and yet securing to the master all that is now expected from slave labor.

2. Rewards for faithful and skilful service; for daily labor well done; for a course of tasks well performed; for contracts diligently and advantageously fulfilled.*

But with all the advantage of the habits and expectations of labor preserved, and of a method of tasks and rewards, there must still be supposed a necessity of enforcement, and of course there must be allowed a power of enforcement, all, subject to the checks and appeals to be named hereafter.

1. If there be any system of rewards, the mere withholding them may be found an adequate enforcement.

2. The Scripture rule, " If any man will not work, neither shall he eat," suggests an obvious method, viz., the rations of the idle may be curtailed.

3. Property being allowed and encouraged, there may be punishment by fines, properly guarded ; not accruing to the master's benefit, save to repair his damage, but to some fund for the advantage of the slaves.

4. Solitary confinement and the whip may be allowed — but reserved, especially the whip, for the last resort — under reference and decision of some authority above the overseer or master.   As in all governments, so it must be understood here, that force is the least available, and has its effect not by being frequent and general, but by being unfrequent and special, — by being, in truth, the last and indispensable resort.

5. There may be added, also, the power of selling against his

---

* Compare Clarkson's account of Mr. Steel's methods.

will a slave found incurably idle and negligent, after due delay and reference.

SECTION II.

Marriage and the Domestic Relations.

Those are bad bonds which are stronger than marriage and paternity. Without the domestic relations, there is no normal condition of society, no right position of human beings. These relations, therefore, must be sustained, in order to well-being. Whatever may be the probable issue of this requirement, it must still be made. In this matter, most surely, evil must not be done that good may come.

In order to the security of the domestic relations, marriage must begin as a civil and religious contract for life, before official persons and witnesses, and with appropriate solemnities ; must be considered as sacred and indissoluble as with the white race ; and must be dissolved only on the same conditions and with the same formalities. The crimes against marriage, also, fornication and adultery, must be under the general laws of the community.

The family thus established must be sacred ; must be protected in its relations of husband and wife, parents and children ; and must not be separated for less causes, or on harder conditions than with the white race.

There will be a direct and blessed advantage to the masters by the establishment and permanence of marriage and the domestic relations, because it secures to the slaves the greatest boon of life, and delivers them from life's greatest evil, in place of the misery now suffered by themselves in the breaking up of families so often occurring, and always so liable to occur.

There must also be an increased advantage from the service of the slaves. Whatever promotes contentment and proper enjoyment ; whatever aids good morals and good conduct, must promote and aid their diligence and fidelity, and must make them more and more valuable so long as their services are desired ; and regarding this matter simply, more valuable if their services are to be sold instead of retained.

Again, there must be some advantage in retaining the arrangement and authority of slavery in promoting and establishing marriage. As in our own state of society, definite and hopeful arrangements promote marriage, and as marriage, held in honor, prevents fornication, adultery, and concubinage, so may it be expected to be among the slaves; while the reverse might be feared, if the accustomed supervision, provision, and hope were broken up. In illustration, if not confirmation, we have the complaint of a friend and advocate of West India emancipation, of the disadvantage of the emancipated population in this very respect; — free, indeed, but too free for the promotion of the marriage relation: "Multitudes of families," he writes, "are growing up almost in the wildness of nature, without the protection of the social condition which is ensured by marriage and its holy obligations. When the people emerged from slavery, the vices of the system, its indifference to the higher obligations of life, its loose morality, its diminished self-respect, and low, sensual condition, still clung to the people."* May we not suppose that marriage would have been better established, and its kindred virtues better secured, and the opposite vices better prevented, if the bond to labor and provision and the general oversight and care had been preserved, than by the spontaneous movements of emancipated slaves, or even of such a free people as the African race must be supposed, if their settlement in the West Indies had been free from the first?

2. On the other hand, if the domestic relations and moralities are sustained, this improvement will react on the value of slaves; either enabling the holder to keep his slave advantageously, or opening better ways than now for the disposal of his labor.

The amelioration here proposed is so indispensable, — in view of the whole circumstances and condition of the slaves, — is such a demand of nature, as to force itself upon the consideration of the South.

"Such a change in our laws," says a writer, years ago, in the New Orleans Bulletin, "is called for by motives of humanity, and an enlightened view of public and private interests. It would be beneficial alike to the master and the slave, to the debtor and the creditor, to the State and its citizens. Strong as is the social tie between master and slave, it would be tenfold strengthened by the adoption of the law proposed." "Slaves in the main would feel

* National Era, March 8th, 1845

themselves more permanent, and become happier and better, rising in the estimation of their masters." "Slave property would become more permanent, and consequently more valuable." . . . . .

The following statement has been lately repeated in many papers. The last New York Colonization Journal quotes it, with favorable comments, from the Port Gibson (Mississippi) Reveille, as follows : —

"The project now being agitated by the people of North Carolina, and soon to be carried before the legislature of that State, is one which, we think, to say the least of it, will create a sensation. It is, 1st. To render legal the institution of marriage among slaves. 2d. To preserve sacred the relations between parents and their young children ; and 3d. To repeal the laws prohibiting the education of slaves. If this modification in the laws is made in North Carolina, as we are informed it probably will, other States will no doubt take the matter into consideration. The main features of the movement have been adopted in practice, or at least approved in theory, by nearly all our planters, so far as circumstances would allow ; and we cannot but think the modification is well worth the serious consideration of every southern man. Should the southern people think proper, after due investigation, to adopt the regulation in each of the slave States, slavery will then be regarded in an entire new light, and the enemies of the institution will then be robbed of their most fruitful and plausible excuse for agitation and complaint. There may be, however, evils to contend with, and objections to be answered, in the adoption of such a modification. We therefore leave the subject open for future consideration, and, in the mean time, invite a free examination of the subject by our readers."

Section III.

Sales and Emigration.

The whole matter of *Sales* comes to be considered in connection with the requirement that the domestic relations shall be established and sacredly regarded. Besides the limitation of sales required by the domestic relations, there may be others needful.

1. It is desirable, if not indispensable, that sales should not be made without consent, except in the case of young children sold with their parents; or orphans of such age that, as free, they would be disposed of at the discretion of their guardians, or the civil authorities. The more nearly this regulation can be adopted, the more cheerful and effective will service be likely to become.

2. There seems needful, at least, a special provision in behalf of young females, whether in view of their actual exposure to the passions of base men, or to those apprehensions and fears which they may feel, making sales against their will the greatest injustice and cruelty. No sales of young females should be made without their own consent and that of their friends, except under due examination and decision.

3. There may be a provision for the sale of refractory slaves, without their consent, under the supervision and decision of the proper authorities; which sale is to be considered as a transportation for misconduct.

If these prohibitions to sales now allowed by law, are made, it is plain that great inconvenience must arise to all classes of the community, whether sellers or purchasers, debtors or creditors. The inconvenience seems so great, that it is generally assumed that the right of indiscriminate sale is essential to the institution; and that it must be valueless without it. We admit the immediate inconvenience, but find in the advantages of a Remedial Code certain compensations, and at length a more valuable use and disposal of slave labor.

1. The use of labor may be supposed to become more easy, secure, and advantageous, by means of the new restrictions on sales. When the domestic relations, and even the wishes of the slaves, are known to be regarded, labor may become so much more valuable, that there will be far less occasion for the sales which now seem indispensable. The relief may be found in the more economical expenditure of a contented service, in the better industry of the laborers, the better cultivation of estates, or their enlargement by the redemption of waste lands. Thus, there may be less debt to provide for, less risk to the creditor, and less damage than would occur if slaves were not liable to " execution for debt," in the present state of things.

2. If the condition of both masters and slaves is made better, **and** if slave labor is thereby more satisfactory, then there may be **less** unwillingness to be sold, and thus an improved opportunity **of sale** by consent, beyond what would be found at present.

3. No doubt, also, when there are occasions for sale, there will be found methods of selling whole families together, by barter or otherwise, with advantage to both buyers and sellers, and with a more satisfactory condition of the slave family itself.

4. Slaves may be made willing to be sold often, no doubt, by a "bonus," given by buyer or seller, or both, or by a bounty proffered in certain cases by the State, to accrue to the slave's advantage, and to be invested for him ; and if with his master, then to be secured on his person, as hereafter explained. In this way it may be hoped that the occasions of buyers will be provided for, either by the consent of the immediate parties sought, or by its general influence upon the labor market at large. Thus under "the fishing bounty," the individual captain may succeed in obtaining the "hands" he seeks ; and if not, will find a sufficient supply in the general market. Thus it may be supposed that even the great western market may find supply. A government "bounty" accruing to the slaves, might be found to furnish voluntary labor, up to the whole demand for western emigration.

5. Under the arrangements for *the property of slaves*, which we have to propose, there is yet another relief to debtor and creditor. The slaves themselves may prevent the necessity of sales, by loaning their own property to their masters, on the security of their own persons up to the amount loaned ; thus relieving their masters, satisfying the creditor, investing their own savings securely, and keeping whatever favorable position they may be enjoying in their master's service.

6. As to the *security for debt* now existing in the liability of sale, the State, if it abolish the existing law on which they were made, must answer for all contracts. When the courts have given judgment against the debtor, the judgment must be levied on the State and not on the master, and the State, if needful, must make such disposal of the slaves as is consistent with the new regulations, and hold itself responsible for any balance which would have accrued to the creditor, if the slaves had been sold without the "*ex post facto*" disadvantage.

7. The new restrictions once enacted, then all contracts would come to be made in view of them, and the business of life would go forward as it now does, under settled legal exemptions. It is no new principle to make exemptions of property, and to have them taken into the account in making contracts. The widow's dower is a long-established instance. With questionable reason, some States have added the homestead exemption.

8. The distribution of estates, except as embarrassed by unfulfilled contracts, may, perhaps, from the first, be required to take its course under the new laws.

9. With regard to the occasions of buyers — to the whole difficulty of getting the service which is needful — in the first place, buyers must submit to the indispensable changes, for the sake of humanity and justice, at whatever inconvenience; while, in the second place, it may be hoped that methods will be found of supplying every needful service within the scope of humanity and justice; and thus with the prospect of better service.

10. With regard to the requirements of emigration, the especial necessity of our extending settlements, at the South as well as at the North: — No doubt there must be at the North, as at the South, a continual emigration of capital and labor, with the desire to improve a prosperous or to repair an impaired condition; and as at the North, so at the South, it must often be with the painful severance of family bonds. But this severance must be on the same principles with the slaves as with the free; must never be with the slaves in such wise as is not tolerated with the free.

Nevertheless, if there be emigration, if the southern West is to be occupied from the southern East, there must be a removal of labor as well as capital — of slaves as well as masters. But let the removal of slaves and the supply of labor be provided for in such ways as the following: —

(1.) Let the removal of slaves be *with* their masters and their masters' children, of them and their children. Let it be a patriarchal removal. Let whole families of slaves be removed, parties being exchanged, by barter or sale, with neighboring plantations, in such wise as to unite families, whether left or carried.

(2.) So far as the good will of the slave is concerned in this matter, and with the general design of furnishing a sufficient supply of emigrating labor for the south-western market, there may be offered, as intimated in reference to the general market, a bounty, which, for this purpose, may be special and larger than for other services, thus securing volunteers ; the bounty, if the slave desire it, to be secured on his person.

(3.) There is yet another method of providing for south-western emigration, viz. : The removal of free blacks as laborers with good wages ; i. e., provided that adequate laborers can be furnished from this class. There must always be a multitude sufficiently needy to be induced by the promise of good wages, to try a new method of life, where, without being enslaved, they may have the opportunity of labor and acquisition, — the provisions and securities which capital alone can furnish.

In order to aid this arrangement, and thus to rid themselves of an ill-provisioned population, as well as make good provision for it, the States, severally, may extend the "bounty" to those free blacks who shall go west as free laborers, under such engagements as will render them available. Such "bounty" might be under the supervision of State commissioners, appointed to make the arrangement mutually advantageous to the employers and employed.

If the West Indies can be at the expense of importing "coolies" for their plantations, or in truth if slaves can be imported from Africa ; or, once more, if the internal slave trade can find a constant market, then surely the purchasers can afford and will be willing to give a "bonus" and wages, such as might be an inducement to large numbers of "free blacks," at once to emigrate and to become available laborers, even without the "bounty" which we have proposed should be offered by the State.

Section IV.

Slaves to be capable of acquiring and holding Property.

The law of marriage being settled, and the domestic relations secured, there must needs be added the power of acquiring and holding property for themselves and their heirs, under the general laws of property and inheritance, with whatever special rules and limitations.

It is understood that the master's claim to service is to remain unimpaired and undisturbed. This, due to the master, for rations and securities, is to be considerad as *owed* by the slave, up to the average value of good and faithful slave labor. And this service is not only owed, but necessary, also, in order that the master may be able to give the rations and securities required; may sustain the capital and arrangements, which, without labor, must become as unavailable to the slaves as to himself. It may be found on trial, on the other hand, that the master's advantage is promoted by the privilege here required for the slave; that his own property will be more valuable because property is allowed and secured to the slave. This will certainly be the case if he is rendered thereby more contented and hopeful in his lot, and more just and generous, in proportion to the justice and generosity with which he is treated. The possession of property, with the protection of the domestic relations, must be conservative in the highest degree.

1. Without any alterations in existing arrangements, there is yet room for slaves to acquire property. Fulfilling their labors as slaves, and returning thus for what they receive, there is even now scope for acquisition for themselves. What we propose is to legalize what already exists, and to extend it to the secure holding, disposal, and transmission of property. This legalized property may be acquired, as extra money now is, by whatever honest means, after the labor due for rations and privileges has been done; by whatever work a slave can do above his allotted work or task; by whatever "bonus" may be given for faithful and successful labors; or, as is now often allowed, the slave may claim the privilege of laboring on his own account, on the security of some responsible person, returning a fixed sum to his master. This is the Russian *obrok*, which proves such a mitigation of the serf's lot.*

2. As capacity and capital increase, so as to prepare them for larger employments, they may be permitted to take charge of certain departments or certain portions of an estate; thus employing and increasing the property which as slaves they may have been able to acquire. They may become, also, contractors for any work within their scope, under some satisfactory arrangement with the master

* Allison's Europe, p. 412.

for service due, and to whatever extent their skill and capital **may** reach.

3. The redemption of waste lands furnishes another obvious **mode** of acquiring property. Slaves may be encouraged to expend their extra labor and gains on such lands, under the assurance that the improvements made shall accrue to their benefit, under some moderate allowance for the bottom, or at some agreed or arbitrated price. A provision for such improvements exists in China. "Any one, by simply applying to government, may obtain permission; and a wise exemption from taxes until the land becomes productive, allows the cultivator to reap a proper reward for his industry." *

4. They may take leases of property, working it with their capital, paying rent for their persons and lands, and having a claim for remuneration for all improvements they make, at a fair and arbitrated rate. To such leases, with security for the improvements made, the comparative prosperity of Ulster is ascribed amidst the miseries of Ireland.† Such leases may be made in perpetuity, if experience should encourage it, as likely to be beneficial to the slaves and the masters alike. The lease in perpetuity of lands and persons would indeed be a virtual freedom, lacking only the rent paid for his own person; and in view of a provision hereafter to be suggested, thus paid, in preference to diminishing his capital by the price of his person. Of the advantage of leases in perpetuity, both to proprietors and tenants, we have illustration in Mr. Colthurst's account of an experiment in Ireland, on two estates under his charge. ‡

Besides legalizing the acquisition of property, it becomes a Christian State, wise and merciful, to encourage and aid its secure and advantageous investment. There are modes of investment implied in the preceding ways of acquisition. The following direct methods are suggested.

1. An open account with the master, and held by the slave, like a savings-bank book; the sums to be on a moderate interest, and secured on the person of the slave, so that if the master refuse or

* Blackwood's Magazine, Oct. 1854, p. 595.
† New York Observer, July 5, 1850.
‡ London Morning Chronicle, January 2, 1849.

fail to pay, the debt may avail to such portion of freedom as the sums loaned might claim; the freedom having a fixed or adjudicated value.

2. Slaves, like freemen, according to their means, may be allowed to purchase any kind of personal property or real estate, and to hold and transmit it as if they were free; themselves still holden to good and faithful slave service, or an accepted compensation therefor.

3. Savings-banks may be instituted within the knowledge and reach of contiguous estates. This has been suggested at the South. The New Orleans Bulletin, April, 1854, recommends it in connection with a fact illustrating the power of present acquisition. A master appeared in court, claiming in behalf of a female slave five hundred dollars, which she had loaned and which was fraudulently retained. Another instance has been reported, of complaint by a slave that he had been robbed of a considerable amount, which complaint was aided by the master's testimony, that he was likely to have had the amount named, and that he had himself been sometimes a borrower from that very slave. Surely, besides legalizing such acquisitions, the State should see that the convenience and security of the savings-banks is extended to the slaves; well assured that neither the masters nor the State will suffer damage thereby.

4. There is yet another mode of investment, viz., *the purchase of freedom;* if the slave prefer thus to invest his savings, instead of keeping them for his present use and comfort, or for greater increase in view of the future occasions of himself and family. Under the amelioration proposed, freedom will become less and less desirable, and probably less and less desired. Still, no doubt, it should be an object attainable by those who may choose to sacrifice its price. There may be, then, legalized an open account with the master, for the purchase of freedom; always available in proportion, if the master should be unable to refund. Or the slave, making his investments in whatever ways he may prefer, may claim his freedom on the payment of a registered or adjudicated price. In the case of partial freedom, obtained by means of debt from the master to the slave, it might be in fractions of a week, as exemplified in the Codrington estate, Barbadoes, under the care of the Society for promoting Christian Knowledge, the slave becoming Monday free, Tues-

day free, &c., until he had acquired the whole six days of the week.

Section V.

Education and Religious Worship.

No doubt the slaves are human, and have a right to all possible advantages belonging to their humanity; are entitled to all possible provision for their wants as intellectual, moral, and social beings. As we fail in regard to the European race, so we may do, in fact, in regard to the African; but there is no just principle of failure with either. Individually and socially, we are bound to provide according to our power for both races alike.

In requiring, then, education and religious worship for the slaves, is it needful to abolish slavery? Or may we not aid and secure these advantages better by slavery retained? i. e., in its essential quality of being held to labor; better than by annulling the obligation and the habits of obedient labor? Whatever answer experience may give to these questions, it is plain that under a Remedial Code, at once retaining and ameliorating their present relation to their masters, both influence and authority will have advantage in aiding and directing the best arrangements.

As every where else, *education* must be understood as including *religious education.* The human being can have no education suited to his whole nature and necessities unless it be religious; not even for time and earth. No education is suitable for man, which does not provide for his right conduct, and of course which does not provide the motives for right conduct; which does not require and aid the inward principles on which men should act; by which temptations may be overcome, evil tendencies checked, and moral wrong and ruin prevented for earth and time, as well as for eternity. If education must be religious, it must also be scriptural; for as Christian men and a Christian people, we have accepted the Scriptures as the supreme guide and authority. In this requirement we provide against sectarian teaching; believing that for the great purposes of this life and the next, *the Bible unexplained* is ample, — that he who is taught the Bible has abundant opportunity to learn his duties to God and man, — his whole guilt and need, and all the grace and goodness which meets him to aid and enable his recovery and salvation.

With religious education, all education should proceed; and this leading the way, all education possible and suitable to the individual will require to be provided for. Reading, of course, is the natural ally and effect of religious education. To this should be added the two other keys of knowledge, writing and arithmetic. All this needs to be legalized, if not required by the State. Without being claimed and enforced by the laws, the repeal of all laws to the contrary would give scope to the conscience and good will of masters and their families, and would go far to promote general education; and so much the more, as the influence and general authority of slavery is retained. Free scope, also, would be given to the general Christian zeal of the country.

There must also be a provision for *religious worship and instruction*. There is difficulty in this, owing to the difference of religious sects. This difficulty must be met, no doubt, with toleration. This being understood, then there is obvious reason for an *actual choice or preference*, for each separate locality; since, while any thing and every thing is waited for, nothing positive will be done. In most cases — the truth being supposed on the whole maintained — the denomination is to be preferred which has already the vantage ground; the encouragement should go with and not against any good current already flowing.

Speaking absolutely and in view of the general wants of the human mind, and of the slaves in particular, there are obvious advantages in a liturgy, — where it can be received with good will, — with which the Church of England is so well furnished. Especially would a liturgy and suitable homilies be of great value on estates, or unions of estates, where there is not a stated ministry. Where there is no such liturgy provided, it is plain that the Scriptures furnish abundant materials for public worship and instruction, — the psalms furnishing prayers and chants.

No doubt there should be provided, as extensively as possible, houses of public worship, for the slaves alone, where they choose it and are sufficiently numerous; but by preference for the masters and slaves together, with no other distinctions than belong to all countries and times, to the relations of masters and servants — distinctions not discarded by the Old Testament or the New.

And will education and religious worship destroy or embarrass the institution ? will it destroy or impair the essential quality of slavery ? will the slave be less easily " held to labor ? "

In reply : Let a Remedial Code be regarded as a beneficial whole. If the ameliorations are really better than emancipation — if the rations and privileges retained with slavery are better to the slave than perfect freedom without them, it is not to be doubted that the best educated will perceive it, and know better than to give up the solid advantages of " rations and privileges " for the empty name of freedom — then bringing no essential blessing to them and their children. The causes of discontent removed, a contented people may be hoped for; the motives to disorder and rebellion no longer existing, the fears of disorder and rebellion may pass away. The masters becoming in truth the patriarchs of the communities around them, the affections and influences which bind them even now together will be strengthened, and mutual confidence prevail so much the more, and not so much the less, as the peasantry are educated intellectually, morally and religiously.

Further, under the ameliorations proposed, active and enterprising spirits must needs find various scope in legitimate ways. The natural desires which issue in establishing the young in domestic life, — the care of young families, now as secure from dispersion as those of the white race, — the attempt for increasing property, now legalized to those still " held to labor," and thereby greater comforts and hopes, — the care of enlarged business to those who become capable of it by growing capacity and capital; and if they desire, the open chance of having *full freedom*, not without but with the means of supplying the lost " rations and privileges ; " — all these will give ample scope and employment to whatever energy and activity, to whatever capacity and education. Still further, there would be opening, continually, various offices of teaching, of religious service and of internal police.

SECTION VI.

The Protection of the Laws : Judicial Provisions and Methods.

The whole social polity of a State has, no doubt, for its essential rule, " Whatsoever ye would that men should do to you, do ye even so to them." The rule for the individual must be the rule for the corporate responsibility, which God holds to account; and all laws should be in harmony with it; no law should contradict it. But this essential rule is to be applied according to right and wise desires, and not to those which are wrong and foolish. It does not require, for instance, parental authority, or the parental states, to abrogate the laws which subject minority, and yield to the wrong and foolish wishes of the inexperienced and self-confident "teens;" for absurd and fatal misrule, though it be in correspondence with the remembered longings of early life. In like manner there is no rule of Christian good-will requiring of the State, laws, provisions, methods for the slave, save as they be right and wise, and not wrong and foolish, in view of their whole condition and relations, whatever we may suppose ourselves to have wished amiss if we had been in their place.

We do not proceed on the supposition that a complete and perfect code can be formed and introduced at once. But endeavoring to survey the whole ground, we must form the most perfect programme that we can; conscious to what imperfection we are liable. Our business must then be to begin with the most obvious demands, and to proceed from step to step as experience and good judgment may direct; assured that no present proposal can foreshow the finished work. With reference to our progress, thus far; the establishment and protection of the family relations, and the allowance and security of property, are obvious demands, which granted, would essentially improve the condition of the slaves, whatever other matters were left unchanged. Certain of the suggestions of the present chapter may be so plain as to claim instant adoption, while others may be questionable in whole or in part, and may require to wait upon time and experience. With this impression, we aim to make our suggestions as complete as we can; providing for whatever special ameliorations, and for the general well-being of the enslaved.

1. The general laws of the State and the provisions for their execution, must be considered as equally for the protection of bond and free; with only such just and merciful exceptions as belong to the mutual relations of capital and labor, still by law retained. If there be any other exception, it should be in favor of the slave, the law providing specially for his aid in any emergency, as the more helpless party.

2. There must needs be a repeal of all cruel and oppressive laws; and whatever cruelty or oppression may have been sanctioned by custom must be forbidden by law. As intimated in Section 1, all summary whipping even, must be forbidden; for if force must still be allowed to compel labor, it will do it with better success when it is deliberate and judicial, and therefore unfrequent. The most effectual penalty for oppression and cruelty of any sort may be the forfeiture of the slave; partly to himself, and partly to some public fund in aid of a Remedial Code.

3. In order to secure justice it is indispensable to admit the testimony of slaves;—it may be done cautiously and experimentally at first; but probably better, instantly and fully, with such conditions as shall best tend to secure its truth. If their testimony must be considered unreliable, it should be remembered that it may become more trustworthy the more it is trusted; and that, at the worst, the tendency of falsehood is always to betray itself and to discover and sustain the truth — giving still the opportunity of right decision amidst false witnesses. This triumph of truth over falsehood has been had a thousand times in the courts of Hindostan, by means of falsehood itself.

4. There may be needed the repeal of laws interfering with harmless liberties and innocent assemblings, which can only be decided in view of circumstances as they are, or may become, in the progress of ameliorations. In general terms, the occasions which seemed to require such laws may be expected to become less and less numerous and imperious, as improvements are made in the general condition of the slaves. A contented peasantry would not need them.

5. There may be required *officers and courts of the slaves themselves*, capable of arresting wrong proceedings, of requiring and enforcing labor from the slaves, and rations and privileges and fair treatment from the master; all checked and restrained by the right of appeal to the higher courts.

There may be conservative, preventive, and even judicial officers — a *slave tribune*, with power to arrest arbitrary proceedings and require investigation; a court of slaves themselves corresponding to a justice's court, with one justice and two assessors, with power to call juries in certain cases; these officers to be chosen from the slaves, and by the slaves, of an estate or contiguous estates, under the power of veto by the master or the courts.

To these arrangements among the slaves themselves there might be added a *clerk of court*, by appointment of the masters, whose business it should be to record, and thus make valid every tribunitial arrest of proceedings; to attend all proceedings of the slave courts, and make record with authentication, before adjournment — at once in security that the proceedings shall not be hasty and inconsiderate, and as a preparation for any needful review.

Some of these suggestions are encouraged by experiments.

"I took," says Mr. Steele, with reference to his estate in the Island of Barbadoes, 1783, "the whips, and all power of arbitrary punishment, from all the overseers and their white servants, which occasioned my chief overseer to resign, and I soon dismissed all his deputies who could not bear the loss of their whips; but at the same time, that a proper subordination and obedience to lawful orders and duties should be preserved, I created a magistracy out of the negroes themselves, and appointed a court or jury of the elder negroes or head men, for trial and punishment of all casual offences; and these courts were always to be held in my presence, or in that of my new superintendent. Seven of these men, being of the rank of drivers in their different departments, were also constituted rulers, as magistrates, over all the gang, and were charged to see at all times that nothing should go wrong on the plantation; but that on all necessary occasions they should assemble and consult together how any such wrong should be immediately rectified." With these arrangements there was also connected a system of rewards with certain amounts of labor. With reference to the effect of the whole, he says: —

"A plantation of between seven and eight hundred acres has been governed by fixed laws and a negro court, for about five years, with great success. In this plantation, no overseer or white servant is allowed to lift his hand against a negro, nor can he arbitrarily order punishment. Fixed laws and a court or jury of their peers keep all in order without the ill effect of sudden and intemperate passions." *

Mr. M'Donough's experiment is thus given by Mr. Sawtelle, in his letter from New Orleans, April 20, 1847, published in the New York Observer, July 31: —

* See Clarkson's "Thoughts," &c.

" The slaves are organized into a perfect republic, possessing all the elements of a free, legislative government. Their trials for misdemeanors and crimes are by a jury, with witnesses examined and special pleadings, with all the solemnities of a court. In important and difficult cases, the old master is called in to preside as judge, and to decide upon some difficult point of law; but the verdict, sentence, and execution are all in their own hands."

SECTION VII.

Franchises and Freedom.

We have proceeded on the assumption that slavery, ameliorated as proposed, is a virtual freedom, while yet the essential element of slavery, the " being held to labor," is retained : the best freedom for the slaves, as a mass, in their actual circumstances now, and for an indefinite future. A Remedial Code is not preparatory to emancipation, but instead of it.

Nevertheless, there may be supposed admissible in the progress of amelioration, first, some extension of franchises to those remaining slaves; and secondly, an opportunity of full emancipation to such as may choose it; thus giving to all some share in providing for their social well-being, and opening the path for individual progress and advancement.

1. The franchises of the mass of slaves, remaining slaves, may be extended, if, in the progress of amelioration, the way should be clear. We have proposed already that they should be able to elect certain magistrates to act in their own affairs. To this may come to be added, on their possessing a certain amount of property, a right of voting (*jus suffragii*) in the State, by means of slave " Comitia ; " their votes having a fractional value compared with the votes of the free; perhaps the same fraction actively, as now passively, in the United States. This fractional franchise might be limited to matters in which their own well-being is specially concerned.

2. There *should be open to all the opportunity of acquiring full personal freedom ;* i. e., the entire release of the slave from being held to labor, with the corresponding release of the master from the obligation of rations and privileges. In this opportunity there may

be a two-fold advantage, viz., of hope and exertion in those who may aspire to personal freedom, and of contentment in the mass; at once in view of the failure of advantage to those becoming free, and the still open way to those who may choose it. Thus it is well that the way to mercantile and commercial enterprise is open to the whole agricultural community of the North, for the like two-fold advantage of hope and exertion on the one hand, and contentment, with the settled advantages of their birthright lot, on the other.

The master may be required to sell at a fixed, agreed, arbitrated, or adjudicated price; and also to keep an open account with the slave preparatory thereto; thus incurring a debt to the slave, available to fractional parts of his liberty as its security, and to full liberty at last. In like manner, all debts of the master to the slave secured on his person, may, for lack of payment, end in a fraction or the whole of personal liberty, whether desired or not.

The fractions of liberty attained might be registered according to law, the master being thereby free from a like fraction of rations and privileges to the slave, and the slave being then entitled to the use of his freed time. If he be sold, it must be under the reservation of his partial freedom.

3. Slaves becoming personally free, must come with reference to franchise into the condition of their class in the States where they reside. If Massachusetts had now slaves to be freed, they would come into the full franchise of citizens; and without damage, if the class remained in its present minute proportion to the whole people. At the South, they must come into the actual condition of their class, and without the franchise of citizens, but at liberty to remove, or to remain contented with their lot, awaiting any changes which time and experience may suggest, — such franchises, for instance, as have been suggested for the slaves in *comitia* for certain purposes, and *communal*, wherever they may form separate communities. If it be insisted that there is no available freedom without full citizenship, it may be replied that the State has done its duty when it has legislated *for* them, though not *by* them; provided their absolute interests have been duly cared for; and if their position is still unsatisfactory, that they are at liberty to withdraw to those States where full franchise is allowed; no doubt to be checked and disfranchised if their ingress should be rapid and great: the sense

of the North being now and then proving itself against *free soil* for large proportions of the African race in their midst.

As to any presumed danger that the numbers of the free would become too great for the interests of labor, and of course of the slaves as well as of the masters, it may be answered, —

Under slavery ameliorated, with families established and protected and property legalized, there must be expected such a regard to the uses of property, to the advantages and comforts which it adds to the rations and privileges of slavery, as will prevent too numerous purchasers of freedom. And this regard to the uses of property cannot fail to be enhanced, by the observation of the free as being often in worse condition than those remaining in slavery, and enjoying at once the provisions of slavery and their own legalized property beside. The present free blacks at the South may themselves come to desire the ameliorated slavery. Besides, if there be proper " methods for the free," then this class may be found more and more fulfilling their part in every department of labor, like the free citizens of the North; and more than compensating any deficiencies caused by the ameliorations of slavery.

Section VIII.

The Methods for the Free.

If freedom should extend to any considerable numbers, there would then be imperiously required some *special methods for the free*, by which their own welfare might be the better aided and secured, as well as that of the other portions of the community. Indeed, even now, at the North and at the South, the necessity of some special methods is manifest; and if this be questionable at the North, it is only because their numbers are so small. Owing to peculiarities of race and condition, there have been found difficulties hitherto, and there is a dread of any considerable increase of the class, not only in the slave States and the free States adjoining, but even to the remotest North. And these difficulties and this dread are not due to slavery merely, but must have existed if the emigration from Africa and the settlement in this country had been free from the first, unless prevented by the wasting of the African race like the aboriginal barbarians. With the race among us, and with experience of the difficulties belonging to them as free, we seek methods suited to the case.

1. Freed slaves may be required, for a term of years at least, to register their names, occupations, places of abode, and the returns of their industry up to a certain amount, and if found vagrant and neglectful may be compelled to labor. As the State must take charge of free, colored pauperism, in lieu of the former masters, so it may take measures to prevent it. No community can be required to confer the right of food, raiment, and lodging, and at the same time to leave the right of idleness and vagrancy, — of want, to be provided for.

2. Under the above regulation, there may be allowed full liberty of settlement and employment.

3. Arrangements in aid of free colored people, such as have been spoken of in regard to those remaining slaves, are desirable; encouraging the acquisition and investment of property. Methods of acquisition and investment should be provided for them.

4. The above being understood, — that they are to have full liberty of settlement and employment, and to be specially aided and encouraged in the acquisition and investment of property, — then, *fourthly*, the employments to which they are accustomed and which are the most open to them, are to be chosen, and are not to be forsaken, without definite and good reason, in the mere hope of changes for the better, any more with them than with the white race when similarly situated. The servile employments to which so many of them have been accustomed, are good employments whether for white or black, whenever useful service can obtain its reward. If they be "low," it is better to continue in them than to make premature attempts to "rise." This is true of any race of people. It is true of those in servile employments of our own people. There must be more reason for the assertion, if peculiarities of origin, character, and race have hitherto consigned the free negroes to those employments; and must have done so, if their immigration and settlement had been as free as that of the Saxon race. Servile employments are good employments when God orders them. And whoever in them, of whatever race or color, is faithful, honest, capable, will find the best elements of well-being; and through them, not in shunning them, the best means — character, friends, facilities — by which to rise, as Providence may open the way, to

those higher employments to which multitudes of the white race never attain.

But this "rising" to higher employments is not the thing to be desired. In large communities there must be servile employments filled by those whom Providence directs. This is not an unrighteous state of society. There is nothing degrading in serving others. "Act well your part, there all the honor lies." There is room, even in enforced service, for the highest excellence and honor. The servants of men, free from "eye service," and "serving the Lord Christ, with singleness of heart and fearing God, shall receive the reward of the inheritance." . . . . . In truth, remaining for the most part as they are, in their accustomed employments, they will find themselves the happiest and most respected, — being more independent, more self-directing, more useful to others, and more capable of reaching something higher, than if they were specially separated from lower to higher employments. In order to be qualified for much, a man must have been faithful in that which is little. This maxim of divine wisdom, true for all, must be more deeply true of a race in degree unimproved and barbarous. It is false charity and false confidence, which is forever underrating servile employments, in the estimation of those who are found in them, and who have yet to prove themselves above them. . . . Let whoever can, by his own exertions and the favor of Providence, " rise," whether he be black or white; but he who shall "be raised," without his own skill and care, and against the provisions of Providence, will but sink the lower for the mistaken pains, whether he be white or black. Barbers, shoeblacks, and waiters, whether white or black, cannot be raised by the talk or hands of others; but acting their part well, so long as they must act it at all, are not low, not debased, not unblessed, but happy and honorable, and in the best way to " rise " to any worthy and desirable height.

5. This claimed, then, let there be every facility for them to rise to independent and leading employments.

(1.) The opportunity of advancement to leading employments should be open to them where they are, as we have claimed already for the slaves, remaining slaves; to do any thing they prove themselves capable of doing, however great the charge and responsibility; and in proportion to their fidelity and skill, they

will rise in respectability and usefulness, without let or hinderance.

(2.) They may be encouraged by " bounties " and wages to emigrate, as laborers in order to improve their condition, becoming thus free substitutes for any slaves withdrawn by the necessary checks upon sale.* They may in this manner be well provided for, and as they may be capable and successful, find leading employments, or become themselves proprietors. . . . . Of course the way will be open, as now, from the South to the North, if they prefer.

(3.) There may be, also, encouragements and facilities for forming free colored communities, as of townships or counties, in which the white race may be discouraged from settling, in such wise as to secure the predominance of the colored race, under the general laws of the States and the United States. Illustrating this, we have the account of a colored settlement at Carthagena, Mercer county, Ohio, briefly as follows : †

In the hope of bettering their own condition and that of their children, some hundreds left their servile occupations in the cities, bought a tract of land thirty miles distant from the source of their provisions. Now (1843) they have many thousand acres of cleared land and comfortable houses, raise their own provisions, manufacture their own clothing, have horses, hogs, cattle, and sheep, and meeting houses and school houses. They have a sawmill and gristmill. The white people respect them as much as they have reason to desire, come to their mills, employ their mechanics, and are employed by them even as day laborers; they buy and sell mutually.

Should such separate settlements be found successful, they no doubt might be extended in the midst of the white population living contiguously on terms of good neighborhood, and with mutual advantage; and the new regions grow with colored neighborhoods, and villages, and townships intermixed; and wherever there were enough to form corporate bodies, they might then be admitted to such communal franchises as the States may award to the individuals of their class.

(4.) A principal method to " rise " must be *emigration to Liberia*, as now under the patronage of the American Colonization Society.

* Compare Section 3.
† New York Observer, August 5, 1843.

This method may be presumed good, and even the best for whatever numbers can find a favorable entrance into the new colony; for whatever numbers may favor a well-ordered community, and shall not outgrow the capacity of self-preservation and self-direction. For limited, indeed, and yet for increasing numbers, it furnishes an opportunity at once for full franchises and all the employments of social life, even to the very highest.

Besides the direct advantage thus afforded, there is also this advantage indirectly. "In large communities there must be servile employments filled by those whom Providence directs." There must be those who work, as well as those who direct and pay for work. The more Liberia prospers and the more numerous its population, the more plain will it become that *it* furnishes no exception to the common lot of men; the more will it appear that freedom on the highest scale, that entire separation from the evils of slavery and from the prejudices of color, does not reverse the merciful as well as just doom, — In the sweat of thy brow thou shalt eat bread; that no more in Africa than in America, can every body have high office and high place, wealth, and ease, and honor; but that the mass in Africa, as well as America, black as well as white, with or without freedom, is still "held to labor," by the necessities of human condition, and by no act of man; checking a thousand foolish aspirations of and for the African race. As Liberia prospers, if their condition be improved in some great essentials of human well-being, it must still become known in this country, and to the African race, whether bond or free, that the toils and difficulties of mortal life, and the distinctions even of masters and servants, are there as well as here; that these are not the doom of slavery but of man — preparing their acquiescence in that ameliorated slavery for which we plead; retaining only the indispensable elements of being "held to labor," and to maintain labor — loosing the bad bonds, and retaining only the good.

CONCLUSION.

Let it be supposed that these ameliorations, prompted by the Southern States themselves, and by whatever suggestions, are faithfully attempted, — the relation of master and slave thus far remaining, that the master is still "held" to provide rations and privileges, and the slave still "held to labor," by which alone provision can be made; marriage established in its sacredness, and the domestic relations protected; education and religious worship provided for; the slaves legally capable of acquiring, holding and transmitting property, and equally with their masters under the protection of the law; and all these with opportunities of freedom, and methods for the free, and we have then a *Remedial Code* in progress and perfecting by experience, suited to the whole case of Africa in America. We claim by such a code,

That the well-being of the slaves is provided for — that they are virtually free; and in view of the actual condition of their race, more free than with the whole franchise of American citizens; better provided for all the purposes of personal and domestic life, than by any general emancipation; and in most cases, than by individual purchase at the sacrifice of property legally their own.

That the well-being of the masters is provided for: the climate and productions of the South, and the original and actual condition of the enslaved race, and long-established customs and habits continuing for substance the present relations of property and labor, — of masters to be honored and servants to honor, with the advantage of greater cheerfulness and fidelity; to the master's joy, more and ever more, in proportion as bad bonds are loosed and good bonds only retained,

We claim, also, for the free negroes, a progressive deliverance from whatever real evils inherited from Africa or America, and blessings in proportion to the blessings of the class from which they have sprung; becoming more industrious and thriving in the midst of a thriving and industrious peasantry, and accepting diligent labor as the best lot of freeman or slave; whether where they are, or, if they will, and when they will, in the land of their fathers, blessing Africa itself in the Christian industry of her retu ning sons.

We claim, also, that in this direction, the conscience and philanthropy, of the country have fullest, freest scope; not in instant remedy of all evils, but in just application of the great Christian law, " Thou shalt love thy neighbor as thyself;" meeting property and labor, slave-holders and slaves, in their mutual necessities and ills, — the suffering "neighbor" on our path not to pass by with indifference, cruelty, and scorn, nor yet with aimless wrangles while we help him not; but with the "oil and wine" suited to his wounds; with the very care he needs, according to our power; supplying the present and providing for the future with generous arrangements and faithful promises.

Nor need we despair of results so great. Whether in view of intrinsic or extrinsic difficulties — of the essential evils of Africa in America, or of reproachful zeal and discordant good-will, and even political anarchy in the strife of equal forces, we may still assume, *The things which are impossible with men are possible with God.* Not that we expect miracles to be wrought, or set forth our hope confessed an enthusiastic dream. Rather do we claim that the whole work of utmost difficulty is within the scope of a common Providence, answering the prayers and aiding the humble attempts of men; not as in the exodus from Egypt, by the miracles of the divided sea, and manna from the skies; but as in the deliverance from Babylon, by the aids of a common Providence, answering the prayers of the captives and blessing the purposes of men; opening " the two-leaved gates," and breaking in sunder the " bars of iron," yet as gloriously " with a strong hand, and an outstretched arm."

POSTSCRIPT Dec. 15. 1855.

*The contest for Speaker illustrating the law of equal forces.**

THE necessity of some new direction in regard to the question of American slavery, was never more manifest than this very day: the United States giving the maximum of illustration of their utter impotence, under the inviolable law of equal forces. If while we write, or at some indefinite future, a minute preponderance shall turn the scale, and our government be organized again, how plainly the law of equal forces will remain, producing impotence again, with only intervals of minute and momentary preponderance ; removing the question of slavery in every form from the National Legislature, and calling for the creation of new powers for new purposes, out of impotence itself. Instead of being shut, the way of wisdom and kindness will only be the more open to philanthropist and patriarch, by the assurance that nothing can be done by authority and power. Instead of being open, the way will only be the more shut, by equibalanced attempts at authority and power. . . .

As hitherto, after every struggle for sectional preponderance, the great questions between the North and the South must take their necessary settlement neither *for* the South against the North, nor *for* the North against the South, but leaving each to their own will and their own responsibility. The great Overruler has so nearly equibalanced them that neither section can prevail over the other. We may try to make the weight heavier on either arm of the balance, but the scales will declare the truth, the moment our hand is taken off. However many may be the librations, the scale must at length settle on the unalterable principles of equipoise. We may quarrel over an impossibility, but we cannot countervail it. As from the beginning useless strife must still give way to leaving matters as they were, — ineffectual and injurious contention to the necessary agreement to differ.

This last struggle, essentially in vain, will not be in vain, if it teach the country the truth forever illustrated by baffled attempts to overrule, on the one side or the other; that God has so settled the equilibrium of sections, that there can never be an overruling

* See Chapter 10.

North, or an overruling South; and if it be felt to the very heart
of North and South, that their only strength in the even-balanced scale is in impotence acknowledged; in *"vis inertiæ"* made
available by wisdom and good will as a reservoir of beneficent
power. The two great sections may influence and aid, they cannot direct and control each other. The labors wasted in useless.
baneful strife, are sufficient to raise a " power " which can work
blessings over all the land. Repeating from the preceding pages,
" Northern philanthropy will do its utmost, not by authority where
no authority exists, not by an imperative balance where there is
an essential equipoise, but without authority, and notwithstanding
impotence, whenever it shall unite an available wisdom to fraternal
good will."

A NEW ERA INVOKED.

December, 1856.

In the Postscript to the first edition of this work, December 15,
1855, when the contest for " Speaker " was but just begun, I found
the United States giving the maximum of illustration of their utter
impotence under the inviolable law of equal forces; and claimed
that only a minute preponderance could turn the scale, that
impotence would recur again and again, — removing the question
of Slavery in every form from the National Legislature, and
calling for new powers, for new purposes, out of impotence itself.

That contest ended after many long weeks in giving the " Speaker "
to the North, in antagonism to the South ; but with a preponderance
so minute as only to make more plain the law which had been

transgressed; with no working faculty; with no available power to give form to intention, to change purpose to enactment; with no majesty of enforcement to give existence and stability to law; impotent to the great work of sectional control, and only fore-showing and preparing the counter-libration of the equi-balanced scale.

Accordingly, despite the utmost efforts to maintain and increase the preponderance, — to give weight to the Northern arm of the balance, — the scale has turned again; yet not less plainly than before, with no decisive preponderance, reasserting and reassuring the *law of equal forces*, which neither Section is able to reverse. The Presidential election of November 4th, 1856, was the consummation of proof that God has settled the equilibrium of Sections, so that there can never be an overruling North or an overruling South; * — that impotence is the only strength in the even-balanced scale, the only element of beneficent power.

At the same time what fearful illustration have we had of the miserable strifes of those whom God has joined together in essential equality, — so much the more miserable because they can neither conquer nor separate, — threatening the lasting curse of the European race, with only evil to the African, who is the subject of the strife. So it happens, sometimes, in that best and earliest society, from which all society springs, — the family. The very elements of equal, inseparable and blessed union, render the life of the parties

---

* It may be asked, Does not the *law of equal forces* produce the same impotence to prevent even the revival of the slave trade, with all its essential wrong, and all its voluntary accessions of enormity ? Undoubtedly it does, — unless the forces shall refuse in that case to be equal. You can make a power with the long arm of your lever, but you can make none when both arms are equivalent. But, inviolable as is the law of equal forces, with regard to the *existing fact* of slavery, I deny that it does or can have place in regard to the renewal of the slave trade. If it were possible to suppose that the suggestions of a Southern governor and of Southern journals, which have just now startled the public mind, should venture to ask enactment and enforcement from the United States, — a living unity only by the provisional abolition of the slave trade in the life-giving instrument itself, — the same causes which in 1787 united North and South, would be effectual again, only in tenfold greater power. The monitions of conscience, in regard to palpable and undeniable wrong, ruling the South as well as the North, — urged by the whole conscience and humanity of the Christian world, — would supply a force immeasurably greater to prevent the renewal, than there was to bring to pass the abolition of the slave trade.

only more wretched, because they can neither rule nor part, **while** ruin befalls the house which each is engaged to sustain.

Under the deepest sense of these lessons and forewarnings **of the year** now drawing to its close, I dedicate this work to-day

TO THE PEOPLE OF THE UNITED STATES,

THE WHOLE PEOPLE,

E PLURIBUS UNUM.

United by separation; powerful over the parts by impotence **as a whole**; weak in authority and power, strong by example and influence; ruling by not ruling; — the foundations of the Pyramid on which the eye of Heaven has looked from the beginning, made firmer by every addition to its weight.

May the librations of the equi-balanced scale, in the year 1856, consummating the proof of the weakness of Sections *against* each other, and of their strength only *for* and *with* each other, inaugurate

A NEW ERA,

in which the whole wisdom of our history as one people, — great, undivided, indivisible, — shall prevail in councils and methods in regard to Southern slavery, as acceptable to the South as to the North, and as advantageous to the African as the European race, in their mysterious relations to each other.

REVIEW

OF THE DECISION OF THE SUPREME COURT IN THE CASE OF DRED SCOTT.

In attempting a review of this decision, on which views so opposite are entertained by two great political parties, the writer does not propose to become a partisan himself. His work, springing up from the germ of 1820,* and growing and maturing until 1856, can have had no connection with the present times, and cannot apply itself to the advocacy of any party without leaving its original and better position as the earnest advocate of principles and methods in which it behooves the wise and good of all parties to unite ; equally suited to the philanthropic purposes declared by the anti-slavery North and to the patriarchal intentions which shall best provide for both races in the slave-holding and slave-held South. It is, then, in the hope of rendering some service in closing the strife, and not as a party in it, that we propose to apply the principles of this work to the Decision of the Supreme Court, for the high purpose expressed in closing the advertisement of the fourth edition, viz. : " To engage the South in their proper work in behalf of the African race, and to unite the North in taking the only position in which they can render effectual as well as acceptable aid."

In brief, the Supreme Court of the United States affirms the Decision of the Supreme Court of Missouri declaring Dred Scott a slave, on the agreed case that he had been formerly a slave under the laws of that State, and that his plea for freedom was insufficient — the Decision being incidentally affirmed, on the ground of want of jurisdiction. This is the simple point, and for our purpose nothing else need be stated.

Keeping in view the principles and design of this work, not only its claim of well-being as the true aim for the African race, but our whole National condition, we say distinctly and solemnly, without reference to the arguments employed by the Court, *The Result*

* P. 16.

reached was utterly and absolutely indispensable, viz. : that the Circuit Court of the United States had no jurisdiction in the case. This Decision was more a necessity of Providence, of HIM by whom the "powers that be" are ordained. than an act at its own discretion as the interpreters of the Constitution. The question at issue was not a National but a State question, by the very ordinances of Heaven, which made us at once separate States and a United Nation, and which, upon the special question of slavery, have so balanced section against section, as to neutralize the power of the United States to enforce the reversal of a Decision of a State Court made on their providential inheritance. With neither authority to reverse, nor power to enforce a reversal, non-interference became a necessity of Providence.

The necessities which made the Constitution, the elements of State and National authority and power, do not depend upon, cannot be set aside by, the legislative and judicial proceedings of the hour. They were, in all their living force, in all their strength of causation, before either the Convention which attempted to abolish, or the Convention which restored and defined the Central and Sovereign Unity of the still separate and Sovereign States, and before the sectional balance had revealed itself, as the necessary result of differences of climate and productions, and of common channels of intercourse and commerce — itself a determined element in "the powers that be." The elements which make the Constitution may be questioned, denied, denounced, but they cannot be annihilated, cannot be deprived of their living and causative strength, of their resulting force. Still it will be true, in the very elements of our existence, by which we are Sovereign States and the Sovereign United States, that we have no authority to annul laws and customs existing in the several States, when we perfected in form our virtual Unity; and as true that we have no power to do it in the matter of Southern slavery, numerical majorities in fact or anticipation notwithstanding. To this end, there are no "powers that be." God has not ordained them. They may be asserted, argued, boasted, but they do not exist, and cannot rule. If there be wrongs, requiring redress, in matters essentially belonging to each Sovereign State when our Sovereign Unity took its form, they are wrongs beyond the legislative and judicial authority of the United States, and in the matter of slavery beyond their power. Whatever might be the intrinsic merits of this case — however gross the wrong by the State Court — the United States had neither authority nor power to redress it. The responsibility was of the part, and not of the whole, of the State of Missouri, and not of the United States.

As to the impotence of the United States to enforce a contrary decision of the Court, let the following suppositions be made, viz. : —

Let it be supposed that the Court had taken jurisdiction, and had decreed the freedom of Dred Scott, the United States Supreme Court reversing the Decision of the Supreme Court of Missouri : —

Let it be supposed further, as the natural result, that thereupon every similar case should make claim to the same freedom, encouraged and aided by the whole earnest philanthropy of the North; and that one thousand, ten thousand, a hundred thousand, for whom a like plea might be made, should demand their freedom from the Courts of the United States, and should become actually, as well as virtually, free : —

Let it be further supposed, that the owners of slaves, thus deprived of their property, as under the laws of their several States, and thousands more, finding their domestics rendered utterly unavailable for some of the most important services required by the well-being of families, should make common cause against a decision so sweeping, and in their view so unjust, and should refuse to obey until the United States should enforce the decree : —

And let it be supposed once more, that the States themselves — one state or more — adhering to their own laws and their own Courts, should protect and defend their own citizens against the Decision of the United States Court, — thus requiring the strong arm of power to enforce the decision.

The question is not now, whether the United States, as a whole, can enforce a decision against a single individual, or a single State, but whether it can enforce a decision which, in its issues, unites the whole South against, though it were, the whole North, on this great sectional question, against the resolved resistance, or even against the resolved inaction, of the South. In this case it is not thirty against one, in which the common consent of the thirty can overrule the one, but sixteen against fifteen, who have compensatory advantages against a nominal majority. Must not the difficulty of executing annul any decree which depends on such an equipoise of power? There can be no available decree, no ruling precedent of the highest court in the land, unless it is sustained by the highest power in the land, and by the common sentiment of the people, by which that power alone can exist. A decision unenforced and unenforceable is as futile, as much a dead letter, as an unenforced and unenforceable law, — dead it may be by anticipation, dead it must be in its result, however it may cling to life. A sectional decision of the United States Court against the sentiment of the whole South, as to its rights and duties, how can *it* be a living and ruling decision? What array of the United States, half against half, can give it vitality and force? When Congress shall undertake to provide the munitions and the men for sectional enforcement, what power will it find adequate to enforce?

In that day of equi-balanced strife, of those librations of the scale which betray the minuteness of alternate preponderance, will not its power be the impersonation of impotence itself? That great Entity, the United States, resistless, overwhelming, when against the single individual or state, what force will it have when it is so equally balanced as to give no determinate preponderance? That mountain rock, which would crush thousands in its fall — when it is balanced on itself, you may put your finger under it and be unharmed.

The impotence of a power so mighty, the non-entity almost of an Entity so august, has ample illustration in the preceding pages. And with reference to the instance in question — to the power to overrule the Decision of the Supreme Court of Missouri, and give freedom to Dred Scott, to the thousands and tens of thousands of Dred Scotts — the power of its presumed librations — we need but shape our questions to those illustrations to make them unanswerable. When, then, the question of enforcement to the supposed Decisions of the Supreme Court, affecting the interests and self-approved rights of the whole South, shall come before the whole United States in Congress assembled, — to provide for sectional enforcement — munitions and men against munitions and men, arisen or threatening to arise, — what overruling power will be found in that all-powerful and sovereign Entity, the United States? What can that equi-balanced assembly do, but react the impotent librations — the struggle and the weakness of equal forces, the powerless days and weeks which preceded the election of a sectional speaker to the thirty-fourth Congress? — ending, if days and weeks, instead of months and years, could end it, " with no working faculty, with no available power to give form to intention, to change purpose to enactment — with no majesty of enforcement to give power and stability to law, — impotent to the work of sectional control, and only foreshowing the counter-libration of the equi-balanced scale." *

In requiring the Decision of the Court, from the necessities which produced and would reproduce the Constitution, rather than from the direct interpretation of that instrument, we give the highest possible encomium to the Constitution itself, if indeed it *is* the actual counterpart to those historical facts which make this nation what it is, E PLURIBUS UNUM ; which give it its distinct and vigorous unity, and its distinct and vigorous plurality. At the same time we give the best justification of the Decision of the Court, if, indeed, as is averred by its opponents, it contradicts previous decisions of the same Court, and even of the very same judges themselves.

No doubt, *precedents*, decisions of Courts of law, have a ruling effect, and will rule until from valid reasons they are themselves overruled. It is not merely by judicial decisions upon the application of laws and their correspondence with constitutional principles, that Constitutions are illustrated and perfected ; but as truly by decisions correcting decisions, whenever, in the progress of events, it may be plain that great principles have been transgressed. Thus the necessities which produced the Constitution have required from the first, and will hereafter require, corrections of previous decisions, in order to preserve Constitutional consistency, and this without making the Constitution the mere organ of uncertainty ; for each new correction can take its place as a reliable precedent, only by conformity to the great principles which originated the Constitution ; — new necessities and new providences only making more plain its original and fixed principles ; the written formula being only better understood and applied in the progress of that course of events *in* which as well as *from* which it took its rise.

So it is with the British Constitution. Neither Magna Charta nor the Bill of Rights, nor both, form absolutely the British Constitution, but those immortal documents along with the whole jurisdiction of the hundreds of years which preceded, and have followed

* P. 119.

them until now, — establishing yet, not Constitutional uncertainty, but more and more Constitutional certainty; precedents at once developing and fixing the principles of the documents themselves. Our written Constitution of 1788, in like manner, has been subject to the course of events — to the necessities which time has made plain — to the decisions of that great Chief Justice who for thirty years explained it as cases occurrent made it plain to himself; and of his assessors and successors on the Bench, leaving with a mass of wise decisions which require no change, some which their own lifetime may have enabled them to correct, and some to be corrected as the application of great principles should be made plain — not changing the Constitution, and making it nothing more than the opinion of the Court for the time being, but developing it more and more by decisions indispensable to its essential and necessary principles, — to Constitutional consistency.

The question is immaterial, then, whether the present decision does or does not contradict some former decision. We are not learned in the "cases," nor have we sought out the precedents. For aught we know or care to know, they may be right who assert that in the case of Dred Scott, the Supreme Court has decided against the Supreme Court, and Chief Justice Taney against Chief Justice Taney. The only question is, *Is this present decision required by the necessities which originated the Constitution, — by the progressive development of Constitutional principles, — by Constitutional consistency? If it be, it is right, and will stand and rule hereafter,* establishing who are the "powers that be," against whatever legislation and judicial decisions to the contrary.

What then, it may be asked, *is* the Constitution? Is it nothing but the decision of the judges on the Bench, as uncertain and contradictory as may be the conflicting decisions of the Courts? Have we deceived ourselves in the airy vision of *the* Constitution, when indeed there was no Constitution at all? no standard, to which all acts of legislation, and all judicial decisions, must conform? As well might it be asked, after hundreds of years, What is Magna Charta? Is it nothing real and substantial, because it has been almost seven hundred years under the same conditions of development and growth, as our "Constitution" for seventy? so enduring and yet unsubstantial? but an airy vision to the sight? On the other hand, its substantial existence is only more assured by its development and growth, until better understood and more truly applied, in proportion as the mistakes of Parliaments and Courts have been corrected, it has become the standard of all laws and all judgments, the deep-rooted and wide-spread " Oak " of the British Constitution. In like manner our Constitution, the offshoot and the growth of Magna Charta in the New World, is not a shadow and a vision, but a reality and a substance, more and still more, because it is illustrated and extended by the decisions of the Courts ; by precedents which remain, because they are the growth and maturity of the Constitution itself — becoming more and more the deep-rooted and wide-spread Magna Charta of the New World.

The Decision being thus required as indispensable by the very elements of our National existence, without regard to the arguments employed by the Court on the Constitution itself, it is yet important to notice the phrase in that argument which has been subject to so much obloquy and denunciation, as denying to the whole African race all the claims of humanity and justice, viz.: " That they had no rights which the white man was bound to respect." This phrase, broad as it is, is not without its limitation, in the argument itself; for certainly *some* rights are implied, and a technical and not general character of the obnoxious expression is required by the clauses, p. 425, " We are by no means prepared to say that there are not many cases, civil as well as criminal, in which a Circuit Court of the United States may exercise jurisdiction, although one of the African race is a party. The question with which we are now dealing is, whether a person of the African race can be a citizen of the United States, and become thereby entitled to a special privilege." Even though thus guarded, it may be to be regretted that a phrase so sweeping should have been used at all, even technically and historically, as it plainly was. Certainly the use that has been made of it, as if its meaning were general and not technical, contemporary and not historical, is deeply to be regretted, because it denounces not the fact belonging to the bench, but the fiction belonging to the denouncers. For whatever be the meaning of the phrase, technical or general, most surely it is not used as expressing the views of the Court or of the present day, but with the utmost distinctness, *historically*, of the times when the Declaration of Independence was made and the Constitution formed, but requiring to be considered in order to a right understanding of those instruments.

Indeed, so far from using the obnoxious phrase, as expressing the opinion of the Court, the Chief Justice implicitly, if not explicitly, disavows it for the Court and the present day. " It is difficult," he says, " at this day to realize the state of public opinion in relation to that unfortunate race, which prevailed in the civilized and enlightened portions of the world at the time of the Declaration of Independence, and when the Constitution was formed ; but the public history of every European nation displays it in a manner too plain to be mistaken." *   Again : " No one, we presume, supposes that any change in public opinion or feeling in relation to this unfortunate race, in the civilized nations of Europe or in this country, should induce the Court to give to the words of the Constitution a more liberal construction in their favor than they were intended to bear when the instrument was framed and adopted. If any of its provisions are deemed unjust, there is a mode prescribed in the instrument itself by which it may be amended ; but while it remains unaltered, it must be construed now as it was understood at the time of its adoption. Any other rule of construction would abrogate the judicial character of this Court, and make it the mere reflex of the popular opinion and passion of the day." †

Surely these extracts show plainly that the phrase in question was not uttered as the opinion of the Court, which may be fairly inferred to be the reverse. For it is given as the opinion of former times, which it is now difficult to realize, and on account of which the race is styled " unfortunate." An opinion, almost obsolete and difficult to be realized, and repudiated in its effects, cannot have been given as the opinion of the Court ; but as the Court itself explains, historically, and therefore needing to be taken into the account in the interpretation of the Constitution, formed when the opinion prevailed. Indeed, if there is occasion for any outcry against the expression of the Court, it is rather for a Southern than a Northern outcry, if, as is alleged, the South maintain the old opinion still. For, undoubtedly, the Court intimate that the present state of public opinion is different, and would require a different interpretation of the Constitution if formed at this day ; whilst yet the language of seventy years ago must needs be interpreted in view of the sentiments prevailing seventy years ago, and not of any changed senti-

* P. 407.   † P. 426.

ment prevailing now, even though entertained by the Court. The judgment of the Court is not declared on what should be the meaning of the language employed, but what must have been the meaning at the date of the instrument itself.

Having made this just explanation of the obnoxious expression of the Court, it must still be admitted that not only the Court but the country, not only the South but the North, do allow to the freed African something less than full Anglo-Saxon citizenship, with all its rights and privileges, as this work has amply asserted and illustrated.* Nor is there the slightest evidence in this wide-spread outcry to the contrary, that either the judgment or the passions of the North would grant to-day the very boon which has been claimed so loudly and so widely of the Supreme Judicatory of the land. The following suppositions may aid in convincing the excited Northern mind that it claims of the Court more than itself is willing to grant, and may prepare the way for those juster views of the difficult problem of Africa in America, which the actual case requires.

Let, then, the supposition, which we have made for another purpose, — viz., to show that it could not be enforced in all its consequences, — return upon us with this change — that it shall need no enforcement — that the decision of the Court, giving full Anglo-Saxon rights and privileges to Dred Scott, shall have free course, with equal consent of the North and of the South, and that thousands and tens of thousands shall receive the boon, increasing largely the number of African fellow-citizens: —

Let it be supposed further, that the South had conceded Kansas to freedom, and that the Missouri Compromise had been unrepealed, and the line of 36° 30′ preserved as the fixed boundary between freedom and slavery ; and that, in order to provide for the Southern free Negroes, now rapidly increasing, there had been established *Southern Emigrant Aid Societies for the settlement of Free Negroes in Kansas,* choosing the most eligible portions of that fertile Territory, and giving endowments in lands and equipments to the whole free black population, both North and South, and that under these kindly aids there should be an emigration by hundreds and thousands : —

* See pp. 21, 22 ; also, pp. 80, 81, 82.

Let it be supposed further, that this African HOST, ready to flood Kansas, should find Kansas too narrow, too distant, and too difficult, and should spread themselves over the States "north-west of the Ohio," and even over Pennsylvania, New York, and New England, as part and parcel of the English race, under the claim decided by the Court, of Anglo-Saxon freedom and citizenship, as the gift of the Constitution : —

Let these suppositions be made as the only natural suppositions in the case, and then let it be asked : —

Will these hopeful and joyful emigrants find, *at the present day*, the welcome from their Anglo-Saxon fellow-citizens, which the present outcry in all consistency requires, and which shall make their co-citizenship a blessing? Those fields of hope, opened to them by the Decision of the Supreme Court of the United States, will they be found opened to them also, by the hearty good will of the people of the North, instead of prohibitory laws and penalties, which shall send them back to slavery, or make their liberty a curse ?

Or, if you will, rather suppose, in all consistency with the benevolent outcry of the times, that they shall be received with open heart and open hand as the moiety of Kansas, and in large proportions in Ohio, Indiana, and Illinois, in Pennsylvania, New York, and New England, how then stands the question before the common sense and sound judgment of the North ?

Is it the deliberate judgment, the well-settled conclusion of Northern philanthropists, nay, of that Northern mass now condemning, by acclamation, the " Decision " of the Supreme Court, that these African immigrants, established in large proportions, as co-citizens, with full Anglo-Saxon immunities, will be found in all respects fitted for their lot, even in their improved state, as compared with their African ancestry, — fitted at once to secure their own well-being in their new condition, and that of the communities whose franchises and opportunities they have come to share ?

What answer does the actual sentiment *of the present day* make? What answer do the Northern settlers of Kansas make? What answer comes from Ohio, Indiana, and Illinois? from Pennsylvania, New York, and New England? Can any one mistake it? Can any one question what would be the outcry, if these suppositions were actually imminent? if the free African blood were even now breaking in upon the hopes of the Anglo-Saxon race? — The

Decision of the Supreme Court — that the African race, though freed, were not considered in the Declaration of Independence, and in the Constitution, as entitled to all the franchises of the Anglo-Saxon race, and that those instruments of our own freedom cannot, in view of the sentiment of the times when they were written, be so interpreted as to require it now, — Would this Decision of the Supreme Court be welcomed or refused in Kansas? in Ohio, Indiana, and Illinois? in Pennsylvania, New York, and New England? Amidst that incoming flood of free Negroes, which we have supposed, would the outcry be for or against the interpretation of the Constitution according to the sentiment of the times when it was made? for or against the practical result of that Decision? Would the flood of freed Africans be welcomed or refused by the *present* sentiment of the North?

There is not the shadow of a doubt as to the answer. Public opinion, after all, has not so entirely changed, as the Chief Justice has intimated; and this " unfortunate race " is not admitted, in these times, and by their best friends, as entitled to *all* the rights and privileges of the " white race," those who are loudest in the condemnation of the Decision of the Court, themselves being witnesses. There is a change, and a blessed one thus far, viz., that they may not " justly and lawfully be reduced to slavery for the white man's benefit."   But where are the classes of men — where are the towns, and counties, and states that are ready to receive them as they find them actually among us, and to give them an equal share, both in numbers and immunities, with the white race?

The facts are as glaring as the noonday.   The laws which have been passed and enforced by the States most exposed to large proportions of free African population, and the reasons given for those laws, show most plainly that there is not " free soil " for the freed African in all our wide America, whatever change of sentiment has taken place as to the right of enslaving. In truth, with but the minutest exceptions, every body thinks — every town, and county, and state, North as well as South — that the African race, improved though they have been since their immigration, are not entitled to be, in large numbers, part and parcel with the Anglo-Saxon race ; that they are not raised to that degree of civilization, of Anglo-Saxon civilization, as to make them advantageously to themselves, or the whole people, parts of the several " Englands " of the New World

p *

not the slaves only as slaves, but the free Negroes also as free Negroes.

And if this be the actual opinion, not only of seventy years ago, but now; not only of the slave-holding South, but of the free North also, with all its zeal for African freedom; and above all, if there is reason for it, in difference of origin, and race, and civilization, such that equal rights and privileges, where the proportion is large, would be for the advantage of neither race, what then is the conclusion? We may deplore the existing opinion, if the opinion be false; we may deplore the facts, if the opinion be just; we may wish that the "unfortunate race" had never been landed on our shores, and please ourselves with the vision of America with a homogeneous people; but after our deplorings and our visions, the opinions and the facts remain; and it is just as true that there is repulsion at the North, refusing "free soil" to the African, as that there is slavery at the South — that "free soil" for the African race is *not* a Northern, as that "slavery" *is* a Southern institution; and the question returns — What, then, is the conclusion?

Is it to deny all rights whatever, not only to the enslaved but to the freed African? to deny all the claims of humanity and justice to the entire race? Is it not rather for the North and the South to unite in the methods best suited to the actual case — not authoritatively on either hand, but fraternally; to take the more pains, to make the more careful arrangement, and to be the more watchful that every immunity due to the actual facts, shall be made sure; that every claim of humanity and justice shall be fulfilled, both to bond and free?

This, certainly, is the honest and earnest purpose of this work; — uniting the North and the South, it aims to give to the slaves something better than the freedom so earnestly claimed for them, and to the free Negroes something better than they would find at the North, if they should come crowding into all the rights and privileges of the Anglo-Saxon race, meeting the humanity and justice which they would find in Kansas; in Illinois, Indiana, and Ohio; in Pennsylvania, New York, and New England. In our "Suggestions for a Remedial Code," we have proposed rights to be acknowledged for the slaves, and methods for obtaining, securing, and recovering those rights. We have suggested also,* "Methods

* Chap. xiii., sect. 8.

for the free," certainly with something less than full Anglo-Saxon immunities, wherever large proportions are supposable — on those reasonable grounds on which none *act* more decidedly than the anti-slavery North. Whatever be the just immunities for bond or free, they are all to be the more carefully provided for, in view of the actual disabilities attaching to the race, with all facilities afforded for every desirable advancement, and all securities for such immunities as may be allowed.

This admission to certain immunities, and not to all, required by the peculiar characteristics and relations of the two races, is not without a parallel and illustration in the history of our forefathers, when there was not the superadded difficulty of a population so remarkably differing in race. You may require Magna Charta to complete itself instantly by giving to the "serfs" all the immunities of the barons of England, but you cannot instantly dispense with the "serfdom," which is the actual arrangement for the necessities of the serfs, as well as for the fuller provision for their lords ; but you may secure all the immunities as well as obligations suitable to the actual conditions of both. You may require the Bill of Rights to give full suffrage to every inhabitant of the British Isles, and such confiscations and distributions as shall equalize the condition of nobles, commons, peasantry, but you cannot instantly give the capabilities and the habits of useful franchise and economical possession, which shall make these immunities a boon to the unaccustomed mass. Or, to meet existing evils, you may require instantaneous relief and comfort for all the cotton mills and mines of England ; to abolish, at a stroke, the whole system of their labor ; but you cannot instantly furnish the indispensable substitute for the method by which the laborers are provided for, and the manufactures of cotton and iron furnished for the wants of millions, the wide world over. In all these cases you might have done and may do more to diminish the evil, and increase the good ; and this is the proper field for your benevolent wisdom.

In like manner, and with more reason, where the population is not homogeneous, and where there is an actual repulsion between the more and the less advanced in civilization, by prejudice or with reason, you are bound to give such immunities as are suited to the case, with the more earnestness and pains, because you cannot give all the immunities of Anglo-Saxon citizenship. You may require instead, slavery to be instantly abolished, labor to be free over all the cotton and sugar fields of the South, but you cannot abolish, we do not say the wants of the whole world depending on those fields, but you cannot abolish the wants of the slaves provided for by the present system of labor, and instantly establish an adequate substitute, nor instantly abolish that terrible repulsion, with and without reason, which forbids them to earn their bread in the whole "free soil" of the North. The cry so common of late, "The world must have cotton and sugar," regards but one part of the case. The men who now cultivate the cotton and the sugar must have bread, — must not find the existing system of labor broken up, without some sufficient substitute, — is the other part. "Laborers must be imported — the peasantry of Europe, 'Coolies' from the East, that the world may be supplied with cotton and sugar;" but this is but part of the case. On the other hand, the laborers of Europe and Asia must *not* be brought in to supply every body else with cotton and sugar, to the lack of the very means of life, of bread itself, to the Africans now laboring the soil for themselves, more absolutely than for the whole world beside. The labor so eagerly sought for, to supply the lack where slavery has been abolished, and where it is proposed to abolish it, how much better is it provided for by the methods of this work, — not by discharging the laborers who now have their claim on capital and land, but by retaining them, with whatever bad bonds loosed, with whatever good bonds added or retained. "Cotton is king." Be it so, and let cotton reign for the benefit of the wide world, neither by perpetuating abuses and wrong, nor by displacing African by European and Asiatic labor, and driving it from the South upon the unwilling and repelling North, but under the MAGNA CHARTA of African well-being.

It is the aim of this work to promote such legislation and such judicial privileges for this present time, and for an indefinite future, as are fitted to the actual condition of the African race, whether bond or free; aiming so high in regard to slavery, that it might be called a regulated freedom, and yet so retaining all advantageous restraints, that it should still be an ameliorated slavery; something "better than freedom" for the slave, "something better than slavery as it is," for the master, with all desirable facilities for individual freedom; and for the freed such immunities and privileges as shall be for the actual benefit of both races, with all encouragement and aid for the fullest enfranchisement in "America in Africa," now opening her arms to receive them.

In truth, *there is but one practicable way, and there can be no other,* in the mysterious relations of the two races in our land, — the method of retaining good bonds only, and of loosing only the bad, — the *method of well-being.* The suggestions made in this work may require variation, the details may be improved by knowledge and experience ; but the principles and the substantial method are as certain as truth, and sooner or later must prevail, if Africa in America, or America in Africa, are to share the blessings of the Christian world. Amidst all the denunciations of existing facts, the strifes of Christian philanthropy, the divisions which have resulted from sectional contention, and the sectional contentions threatening still further divisions into churches North and churches South, benevolent societies North and benevolent societies South, what other method is practicable? Nay, amidst these earnest debates, as aimless as earnest, what clear and distinct proposal is made? What other daylight dawns upon the night of our perplexity? Who will tell us, not of any thing better, but of any thing else that can be done, not only *with* but *for* the mass, the millions in our land?

Shall they be set free, with full liberty to flood the North? Alas! it is one thing to denounce slavery, and another thing to receive the freed slaves with mutual advantage ; one thing to keep up an outcry against the " peculiar institution " of the South, and another to accept multitudes of African freemen as the new " institution " of the North. It is one thing to pass a few fugitive slaves through and beyond your State on the " Underground Railroad," and another thing to receive crowding multitudes to your houses and lands, to share favorably or not, for them as well as yourselves, all the opportunities of enterprise and livelihood with your families, if it be not rather to live upon your scanty charities, or be absolutely repelled by your electrical touch.

Or shall they be set free and *kept* South? — free, and yet not free — emancipated into bondage — obliged to stay under disadvantages which they feel, and forbidden to go to the advantages which seem to them so great ; with no claim upon capital where they are, and no liberty to seek employment among the friends of whom they have heard so much? And shall Southern capital be compelled to maintain them after that disorganization of existing arrangements which forbids them at once to compel labor, and to compel from the ground the means of sustaining labor, when itself shall cease to be " capital," and to have any power of sustaining masses more miserable than homogeneous Europe has been able to show?

Or, yielding to the South its providential and constitutional right to retain slavery where it is, but claiming both right and power to forbid its extension, will you restrain it within its present limits, and forbid its existence over your whole wide, unsettled domain? Admit, contrary to the arguments of this work, that you can do it, are you prepared for the method you adopt? — for the results of that embarrassment with slavery, and the enforced freedom which you expect at the South when the outlet ceases, when, as you predict, slavery shall cease because it can no longer subsist on its worn-out fields, and the doomed South shall be free of its capital and labor, of its masters and its slaves, and the pent up flood shall at length burst its barriers, and roll over your " free soil " in distresses and numbers beyond your provision and control. The very issues you predict, would you be ready to meet them now, or are you willing to entail them upon those who shall come after you?

If, then, the South *cannot* keep them save by means of labor to employ " capital " and capital to employ labor; if the North *will not* receive them when made free according to its call, but only repel them, what else can be done but for North and South to unite in promoting their well-being? Who can forbid the assumption, bold as it is, There is this way, and there is no other? *The assumption must abide its time*, and will prove itself vain unless it is founded in reason and truth, in the nature of the case, in the relations of men, in the wisdom of Providence, in the principles of Christianity, and in the best hopes for time and eternity proffered to every race and condition of men. *The writer believes that his work will stand this test ;* that its principles and methods will more and more commend themselves to the minds of men by their intrinsic merits prior to experience, and will more and more gain ground by their adaptation to the actual case and to new emergencies, by the impossibilities which will arrest every other attempt, and by the facilities which will be found in that which is as true and right as it is practicable and fitting. To the writer, the principles and methods of this work seem to have the certainty of science; to be axiomatic and consecutive in the highest degree ; to be as sure as the truths of Christian good will and the certainties of Providence above the devices and powers of men. They may be questioned, refused, denounced, but are sure to prevail, whether by wise anticipation or bitter and prolonged experience. Dream what we may, devise, attempt what we may, question, refuse, denounce what we may, *There is this way, and there is no other.*

As to the difficulty, whether of engaging the South in the work of amelioration, or uniting the North in the only position for fraternal aids, — the latter, it may be, greater than the former, — we return to the assurance of our Preface of 1856 — THE THINGS WHICH ARE IMPOSSIBLE WITH MAN ARE POSSIBLE WITH GOD.